OVERCOMING OVERWHELM
Journal

A 12-week wellness
planner for finding
peace in a busy world

BEX SPILLER

DAVID & CHARLES

www.davidandcharles.com

CONTENTS

HELLO AND WELCOME!

It seems strange to say 'I'm so pleased you're here', because I know the reason you're holding this book is that you're overwhelmed. *But*, I am really pleased that you're taking steps to overcome that overwhelm. The first steps are the hardest and I know how challenging it can be even to make those. I've been in the depths of overwhelm – bursting into tears at the tiniest of things because I just couldn't add anything else to my plate. Trying to untangle everything and move forward felt overwhelming in itself, so I know what a huge step even just buying this journal is.

This is the journal that I wish I'd had all those years ago when I couldn't ever see a way out of the never-ending to-do list. If it helps just one person feel less overwhelmed, then that's a job well done in my eyes!

I learnt a lot when *The Anti-Burnout Journal* was published in 2022 and while the feedback was amazing, I knew we needed more space for brain dumping and flexible planning. Whether you've completed *The Anti-Burnout Journal* or this is your first journal from me, I'm really grateful for all of your support and I'm always here for your feedback. You can find details of how to get in touch with me at the end of this journal, so please do share your journey with me (I also love photos!).

Right, enough about me, you're here for you. We're about to go on a journey together to clear our minds, untangle the chaos, and begin to breathe more easily. We'll start with a look at how to use this journal – don't skip this bit, it's super important. Then there are three parts (or chapters if you like) with journal space in between. You can read one part a month, all three parts in one go, or spread it out over the year. It doesn't matter how you do it, what matters is that you make it work for you.

Wishing you all the best on your journey to overcoming overwhelm. I'm rooting for you!

Bex x

A QUICK GUIDE TO BRAIN DUMPING AND USING THE JOURNAL

This journal is based around one of my favourite ever tools for overwhelm: the humble 'brain dump'. Brain dumping is something I first read about in Brian Tracy's *Getting Things Done*, and a tool which I have adapted and refined over the years to make it work specifically when I'm feeling overwhelmed.

Throughout this journal, you'll find weekly brain dumping pages which will allow you to dump everything out of your head and down onto paper. Research shows that we find it much easier to process things when we write them down. The simple act of putting pen to paper can really help us untangle our minds and start to clear some of that constant noise in our brains that overwhelm can cause.

The fact is, our brains (however amazing they are) simply can't hold on to all of the information we keep feeding them day in, day out – all of the reminders, to-do lists, important dates, fun facts we discover when going down Wikipedia rabbit holes, and that really addictive song you heard on TikTok once.

If you've ever been brushing your teeth and suddenly remembered Aunt Susan's birthday is tomorrow, or that you need to add bread to the shopping list, then you're not alone. It's in these quieter moments, when we're often on autopilot, that our brains like to remind us of all the things we have forgotten. And don't get me started on the middle of the night reminders either!

Throughout this journal, I really encourage you to get those thoughts out and start processing all the noise in your head. But how do we brain dump to ensure we're not just adding to the overwhelm with ever-growing to-do lists? Here's my step-by-step guide to using the brain dumping sections of this journal.

MAKE IT ROUTINE

First up, I highly recommend you pick a day and time that you'll brain dump every week. For me, it's Sunday evenings when those Sunday scaries start creeping in. For you, it might be Monday mornings or even the middle of the week. It really doesn't matter when, what matters is that it's a time you can keep the same each week. You'll want around 30 minutes to go through the whole process – although it can be longer or shorter, depending on how much you have to untangle.

START BY DUMPING IT ALL OUT

To begin the brain dumping process, start by writing out every single thing that's in your head. And I do mean everything! It could be important dates or appointments to remember, to-do lists, people to call, or even worries and thoughts that are taking up brain space. Let it all out! This may feel a little difficult, especially if it's your first time, so don't be afraid to stop and come back to it as things start to pop into your mind. I find that I'll start my brain dump on a Sunday night but am still thinking of things to add to it on Monday morning – and that's okay!

You'll find two different types of brain dumping pages throughout this journal: one big double-page spread at the end of each part or chapter, which is perfect for monthly brain dumps; plus, a smaller one-page brain dump at the end of each week.

START SORTING THROUGH

Once you feel as though your head has been emptied as much as possible, you'll likely be looking at what seems to be an enormous to-do list. At this point, the panic might set in. 'When will I ever find the time to do all of this?!' Please don't worry. As we start to sort through and categorise things, you'll start feeling more at ease. The overwhelm might just feel a little worse before it starts to get better. To sort through your brain dump, I recommend approaching it in the following order (although feel free to adapt this in a way that works for you).

DATES AND APPOINTMENTS

Any important dates and appointments that you have to remember should go on a calendar, or be scheduled into your journal, right away. These are very quick items we can sort immediately and then start crossing off our big list.

A little note on crossing things off the main list, by the way...

It's down to you how you want to do this, but for me, I like to highlight or star them once I've sorted and scheduled them. I then highlight with another colour or tick them off once they've been completed. This helps me to keep track of what still needs to be sorted through and scheduled, and what still needs work.

QUICK WINS

I then like to see if there's anything on the list that can be done this very second. By which I mean anything that will take just a couple of minutes and can give me the positive dopamine hit of ticking something off straight away. Even if it's just adding bread to the shopping list or sending an email, look for a couple of quick wins that you can get under your belt as soon as possible.

CATEGORISING THE BRAIN DUMP

What's left on the list? Probably a lot of random to-dos from all the different aspects of your life. There may be general things to do with work or specific work projects, tasks in your home life and social life, personal and health issues, and perhaps jobs for family or children too. This is where it gets personal, because you'll define the categories that work best for your brain dump.

On the categories page, write out the different areas of your life that you want to split your brain dump into. So many of mine are often work-based, so I split them into the different projects I'm working on, plus one for home and personal. You may have more home- and personal-based ones, so will want to split that category into different aspects of that part of your life.

Scan through your brain dump and see which categories work best for you. Bear in mind that you don't have to stick with the same categories every single week. You can change these week by week, depending on your ever-changing responsibilities.

Once you've got your categories, start moving items from the brain dump into the relevant category. And again, you can highlight or star these to show that they've been sorted through and/or scheduled.

SCHEDULE THEM IN

Now you've dumped everything out of your head and sorted through it, it's time to actually schedule everything. You'll find daily pages to help you plan out your to-dos throughout the week and throughout this journal. I'll also be helping and guiding you through different ways you can tick these things off too.

My top tips for scheduling in your to-dos are as follows:

* Focus on three main priorities for the day. We can often overwhelm ourselves by trying to tick too many things off in one day, so consider what the three biggest to-dos are today, and how you can get those ticked off. Anything else completed that day is a bonus!

* Leave yourself breathing space. The reason the daily page is split into morning, afternoon and evening instead of specific times, is to give you more fluidity and breathing space to get tasks done. It can be really demotivating to pack your schedule hour by hour and then have something overrun and ruin the whole plan. If you have a specific appointment then of course write the time down, but for the rest of your tasks just consider whether you want to complete them in the morning, afternoon or evening.

* What time of the day works best for you? We'll go into far more detail about scheduling tasks at specific times of the day further along in the journal, but for now consider when you feel most productive and able to complete different things. The Anti-Burnout Matrix in Part Two is perfect for this.

* Try not to schedule too far in advance. You may want to schedule your whole week of to-dos in your journal as soon as you've finished your brain dump, but I generally don't do more than one or two days at a time. Why? Because if something overruns or has to be postponed for whatever reason, it ruins my schedule for the rest of the week. You may want to have a rough idea of what you'll complete when, but again give yourself some breathing space for any unplanned obstacles.

DAILY PAGES

As already mentioned, you'll find space to schedule your to-dos and your top three priorities each day, but there are also other parts of the daily page to consider too.

ANY CHALLENGES I MIGHT FACE

The first is to consider any obstacles you may come across when trying to complete your to-dos that day. One way we can really plan ahead is almost to second guess anything that might crop up during our day that could throw us off course. This could be something we face regularly, like mobile phone notifications; or a particular obstacle you're concerned about that day, like feeling tired after a long meeting. Write down any challenges you might face that day before moving on to...

HOW I'LL OVERCOME THEM

Once you've thought of any challenges you might face, jot down one or two ways you may be able to overcome them if they crop up. Perhaps you'll turn notifications off so you can get some things ticked off the list, or you'll plan a break after that exhausting meeting, to reset. You may not face any challenges throughout the day, but if you do then at least you've already planned out how you can overcome them.

MOOD TRACKER

It's important that we check in with ourselves often, especially when we're feeling particularly stressed or overwhelmed. Use the mood tracker in the morning and the evening to monitor how you're feeling. You may also notice that there are patterns or events that trigger a low mood for you. Recognise how you feel, without judgement, and see if you notice anything that often turns your day from a good to a bad one – or vice versa.

END OF DAY CHECK-IN

Finally, check-in at the end of each day. Reflection is such an important part of dealing with overwhelm, so write out the things you're proud of, what you've learnt, and your gratitudes for the day. We can often focus so much on the bad, stressful things that happen throughout the day that we forget some things have actually gone our way! Use this space to practise gratitude and celebrate your achievements.

END OF MONTH CHECK-IN

At the end of each month you'll find some reflection pages to help you focus on bringing balance and shifting anything that's not working for you. The end of month check-in is set out as follows:

ACHIEVEMENTS FOR THE MONTH

Let's celebrate all the things that went well for us this month! List your top five to ten achievements for the month, big or small. It could be anything, from not forgetting about the clothes in the washing machine (guilty) through to getting a pay rise at work.

WHAT DIDN'T GO SO WELL?

The little box underneath the achievements section is for jotting down any notes on things that may not have gone to plan this month. Approach this gently and without judgement as much as you can. Not everything goes well and that's okay, use this space to reflect on what you've learnt as opposed to putting yourself down.

YOUR WHEEL OF LIFE

We'll then move onto another one of my favourite tools – the wheel of life. This visual prompt helps us evaluate which areas of our life are going well and which ones may need a little bit of TLC. If one area is really lacking that month, consider what you may need to help rebalance.

CARRYING FORWARD YOUR BRAIN DUMP

Next we'll look at any tasks that you've struggled to complete. We can sometimes get stuck on certain to-dos that can then make us feel overwhelmed as we just can't seem to get them done. If you find yourself moving tasks from one week to the next, it's important to reflect on why. Write down anything you've been putting off or feel stuck with. Then spend a little time thinking about what is making you feel this way. Dig deep, the answers may surprise you!

LETTING GO AND MOVING FORWARD

Finally, you'll decide if any of the tasks you're stuck on are things you need to let go of. Maybe they're not a priority for you anymore? That's okay, move them to the 'task to let go of' column and remind yourself why you need to let go. Anything that does need to be carried into a new month goes into the 'task I want to prioritise' column as a reminder that it's important for you to complete them next month. You've also got space to write out your plan to achieve those things you're putting off.

As we go through each part of the journal, I'll be sharing more tips and advice to help you untangle your mind and stay on top of your to-dos and tasks. *But*, one important thing to note, please don't overwhelm yourself trying to do it all. Work through the journal at your own pace. This journal is undated for a reason! If you miss a day, week or month, don't feel as though you've failed and leave the journal gathering dust on your shelf. Come back to it as soon as you feel able to and just continue from where you left off. There's no failing or falling behind here!

PART ONE:

Understanding Overwhelm

––––––

Before we start to untangle our minds, we
have to work out what's causing them to
get tangled in the first place. Let's begin to
understand our beautiful brains.

Overwhelm is something that all of us will experience at least once in our life, and, for many of us, something we'll experience a lot more than once. When we become overloaded with an ever-growing to-do list, it can feel as though we're sinking deep into the water and we don't know how to swim back up.

We start to think, 'Should I be trying the doggy paddle first? What about the butterfly? Maybe a breaststroke will help?!' It's as though our thoughts have become impossible to untangle and we just don't know how to move forward. Overwhelm can lead to 'analysis paralysis' and instead of picking a way to swim up to the surface, we go over and over in our minds what stroke would be best to start with.

If any of this sounds familiar, then please know you're not alone. There's a reason the Overcoming Overwhelm course we ran at The Anti-Burnout Club back in 2021 quickly became the most popular course we'd ever done. That feeling of overwhelm is one shared by many and, when we're in the depths of it, can feel impossible to get out of.

Consider this journal your lifejacket. You're still going to need to do some swimming, of course, but it's going to give you the time and the space to untangle your mind and pick the right way to swim to safety.

There are three parts to our Overcoming Overwhelm journey: understanding it, untangling our minds, and then techniques to reduce overwhelm when it strikes. We're starting with understanding overwhelm, because I'm a big believer in the phrase, 'knowledge is power'. The more we understand that these thoughts, feelings and emotions are a normal part of being human, the quicker we can stop judging ourselves for experiencing them in the first place.

If you've ever felt as though you're 'useless' or a 'failure' for not being able to keep on top of it all, then hopefully this first section will help quieten down that negative self-belief and help you focus on what really matters – getting out of the water!

THE CYCLE OF OVERWHELM

Daily life is noisy, even more so now we have technology vying for our attention as well as all of the other day-to-day responsibilities. The speed at which we live our lives is so much faster than it was even just a few decades ago, and it can feel practically non-stop. As soon as our mobile phone pings, we feel as though we have to deal with that right away lest it becomes another thing on the ever-growing to-do list. We get caught in a loop of dealing with the 'urgent', pushing other things aside, and then feeling as though we'll never catch up.

When we're overwhelmed, it can seem as though that noise will never go away; we'll never clear that to-do list and we'll be stuck in that loop forever. The things that often get pushed to one side when we feel like this are the things that we see as selfish or not worth our time right now. For example, looking after our own wellbeing or taking time to rest and recuperate.

We may hear ourselves say, 'How can I relax when I just have so much to do? When the to-do list is cleared, then I'll focus on me again'.

But the cycle continues, the busyness doesn't stop, and the things that would likely help us are the things we push to another day as we focus on clearing that to-do list. We get stuck in 'doing mode' and this, in turn, can make the overwhelm so much worse.

When I was at the peak of my burnout and overwhelm, I didn't feel as though I could switch off from all of the noise. I was answering work messages on my wedding day and saying to myself, 'That's fine, at least it'll be less to deal with when I'm back in the office'. Except there wasn't less to deal with, and I missed vital parts of the best day of my life because of the fear of sinking.

WHAT CAUSES OVERWHELM?

So, we've already established that technology can play a big part in us feeling overwhelmed nowadays. However, that doesn't mean that locking your mobile phone away forever will solve all of the issues. There are many reasons why we might feel overwhelmed. See how many of these you can relate to:

· A heavy workload and too many responsibilities, at home or at work
· Demands from work or family that we feel as though we can't say no to
· Feeling as though there aren't enough hours in the day to get everything done
· Life transitions and changes, such as moving house, changing jobs, or divorce
· Issues in relationships and/or friendships that cause emotional strain
· Traumatic events such as bereavement
· Underlying health conditions, both mental and physical, that can make it harder to stay on top of everyday tasks
· Fears and anxieties that we're worried we can't handle
· Worries for our future and security (for example, financial worries)

What I've learnt over the years is that everyone will have their own reasons for feeling overwhelmed and none of these are more or less worthy than anyone else's. We all have our own personal limits and what might seem like an 'easy life' to one person might feel practically impossible to another. Never judge your limits against anyone else's – it's always all relative.

I really recommend you pause for a moment now and consider the reasons you might be feeling overwhelmed. Make some notes if you wish. What's going on in your life that may be making you feel particularly stressed right now? Remember, it's important to bring these to mind without judgement. Feeling overwhelmed doesn't mean you're useless or a failure, it's all part of being human. So, consider what may be causing your overwhelm and if any judgement pops into your head, simply reassure yourself that it's okay to feel this way. You're not failing, you're not useless, you're just human.

NOTES

CONDITIONS OF WORTH

Another potential cause of overwhelm is something I learnt from the wonderful integrative therapist, Gemma Curtis, during The Anti-Burnout Club's Overcoming Overwhelm course. When Gemma explained this theory, things started to fall into place for me. It became clear that much of the root of my overwhelm actually stemmed from something most of us have very little control of—our 'conditions of worth'.

The premise is that many of us have expectations of ourselves that come from authority figures in our lives, whether they be parents, teachers or people we look up to, or even society and our culture as a whole. These people will instil their values and beliefs in us, which then leads to our conditions of worth. For example, 'I am only acceptable in society if I work really, really hard'. Or, 'I am only lovable if I say yes to anything anyone asks of me'.

Most of us will have these conditions of worth ingrained in us without even being aware of them, and they can leave us feeling like we 'should' be doing a lot of things that perhaps we don't even really want to be doing. When these 'shoulds' pile up, it can lead to feelings of overwhelm.

I realised that my own conditions of worth had created people-pleasing tendencies, perfectionism, and the mindset of 'if you're not working all hours of the day, you're being lazy'. These are things that had been instilled in me, subconsciously, through the authority figures in my life. They led to me feeling as though I wasn't good enough if I didn't work myself to exhaustion, say yes to everything anyone ever asked of me, and make sure that everything was perfect.

Consider what values and beliefs have come from society, culture, and authority figures in your life. Jot them down if you wish. Do these match the values and beliefs you hold personally? Are there any things in life you feel like you 'should' do because of someone else's expectations?

These questions should be approached without judgement and may even be something you want to work through in a therapeutic session. However you approach them, I think considering these questions is so important in helping us to get a deeper understanding of why we may find it hard to say no or put unrealistic expectations on ourselves.

COMPARISONITIS

Following on from conditions of worth, there's another reason why we might feel overwhelmed, which is, again, something we may have learnt subconsciously. How many times have you scrolled through social media or watched a TV show where you thought, 'How on earth do they keep it all together like that?!'

It might even be a little closer to home – a neighbour, a parent at the school gates or someone you work with. We can often encounter people in our lives that give us an unhealthy dose of 'comparisonitis'. We wonder why we can't have the seemingly perfect life that they have and how they manage to juggle it all, and that sets off all kinds of insecurities.

Many of us can feel overwhelmed when we compare our lives to those who apparently have it all together. We look at those who just seem to be on top of things and think, 'How can they do it, but I can't?!'. We often think there's something wrong with us.

It took a long time for me to realise that what we see on the outside, isn't necessarily the reality of the situation.

When I was studying for my postgrad at Warwick Business School, I made friends with one woman who, in my eyes, just seemed to have everything. She was super successful in her career, she already had a Master's and a PhD under her belt, and she was a real gym bunny with abs for days. I just couldn't work out how she found the time to do everything and I felt so inferior, barely holding my own life together when she was achieving so much.

However, after many long chats with this real-life 'Wonder Woman', I realised that things weren't always as they seemed. We became great friends and the more I learnt about her (outside of what she posted on social media), the more I realised she was just like me – overwhelmed and just trying to keep everything together.

Before you compare your life to someone else's and begin to feel overwhelmed, remember that a lot of what we see is just a snapshot in time. Very few of us show what's going on behind the scenes: the messy houses, the tired eyes, or the never-ending piles of washing.

NOTES

WHAT HAPPENS WHEN WE'RE OVERWHELMED

Whilst feeling overwhelmed is a normal human reaction, that doesn't mean it's something we want to deal with for the long term. And actually, it's not good for us to be in a constant state of overwhelm and stress. When this happens, we can find that it impacts many other areas of our life.

POOR SLEEP

Probably one of the first things to be impacted for me when I'm overwhelmed is sleep! You may find that you see changes in your sleep pattern, whether that's not being able to get enough sleep because your mind is racing, or sleeping more than usual because you constantly feel exhausted. Sleep can be a real catch-22 because getting good quality sleep can really help us manage stress and overwhelm... but, if our sleep is impacted by overwhelm, then it can be a vicious circle that we struggle to break out of.

PROCRASTINATION AND ANALYSIS PARALYSIS

Just as I mentioned right at the very beginning of this section, when we're feeling overwhelmed we can struggle to make decisions or know how to move forward. You may feel as though you have 20 plates spinning at once and you don't know which one you should handle first. This leads to procrastination and the act of being 'busy' all the time, but not actually feeling very productive. A big part of this journal is about untangling our minds so that we don't get stuck in procrastination and analysis paralysis mode.

GETTING STUCK IN THE 'CATCH UP' MENTALITY

How many times a week do you think you say 'I need to catch up' on something? Whether it's something at work, in your home life, or even journaling – getting into the 'catch up' mentality can be a slippery slope! Every day that you start in the 'catch up' mentality is a day you're subconsciously telling yourself you're behind. Sometimes before we've even got out of bed! If you go in with the mindset of believing you've fallen behind, you instantly feel as though you're on the back foot and tasks become harder and harder to do. It can leave us feeling stuck. Anyone who knows me or has been part of The Anti-Burnout Club for a while knows that I ban the phrase 'I need to catch up'. Instead, I appreciate that whatever I'm 'behind' on wasn't a priority for me at that moment in time and I can simply reprioritise it to whenever suits me best.

HIGHER LEVELS OF STRESS AND ANXIETY

Probably the most obvious and detrimental thing that happens to us when we're overwhelmed is the constant feeling of stress and anxiety. We feel worried that we'll never be able to catch up, and stressed that it all seems too much. Our bodies feel as though they're in constant fight or flight mode and our sympathetic nervous system (the part of the body that activates the fight or flight response) goes into overdrive.

Not all of these feelings are bad, though. Humans need stress and anxiety to keep themselves safe and thrive. Small doses of good stress and anxiety can help us give our best at job interviews, to not cross the road without looking, and even to get that book finished on time (or so I keep telling myself).

But when we're constantly overwhelmed, we experience higher levels of stress that can impact our health in the long term. I won't go into what happens when our bodies have to contend with chronic stress, as I don't think that will help with anyone's overwhelm right now! However, a quick online search for those curious should give you all the answers you need. The bottom line is that constant feelings of overwhelm aren't good for us. You know that, I know that, and that's why we're here making a plan to move forward. Right now, you're in the best place you could possibly be.

SO HOW DO WE MOVE FORWARD?

This journal has been split into three key parts – and we're already coming to the end of Part One. Congratulations! I know how hard it is to concentrate on anything other than the ever-growing to-do list when you're feeling stressed and overwhelmed, so consider this a huge achievement. You're getting closer to less noise and mental clutter, which I know is a huge relief in itself.

In Part Two: Untangling Your Mind, we'll look at how we can deepen our brain dumping practice, create schedules and routines that work, and I'll give tips for decluttering your space and mind. This is where we'll really start to feel organised and in control.

Finally, in Part Three, we'll look at even more ways to overcome overwhelm beyond journaling, scheduling and routines. We'll look at what to do when you're feeling stuck, habits that can help reduce overwhelm for good, and round up everything we've learnt with some top tips.

It's down to you how you want to proceed now. You can spend a month getting into the routine and habit of journaling, using the brain dumping, daily pages and reflection sections, before moving on to Part Two. Alternatively, you might like to read through each of the parts first and then start journaling. This is your journey and it's entirely up to you how you'd like to take it. Whichever way you pick, I wish you the best of luck in your overcoming overwhelm voyage!

You're about to start the brain dumping process and journal pages, so here's a quick refresher on how to use the journal:

- Brain dump everything out of your head and onto paper
- Anything with a date goes straight onto a calendar (or in the journal)
- Quick wins should be ticked off ASAP
- Everything else gets sorted into categories of your choosing ready to schedule for the week
- You've got a bigger brain dumping section at the start and reflection pages at the end of each part (good for monthly brain dumps), plus smaller weekly brain dumps
- Use the journal pages to plan your priorities and daily tasks, track your mood, and reflect at the end of each day
- Take it at your own pace and make it work for you!

BIG BRAIN DUMP
PART ONE

SORT YOUR BRAIN DUMP INTO CATEGORIES

Fill in your categories, then move everything from the main brain dump list into its category.

Category:

Category:

Category:

Category:

Category:

Category:

Everything else:

MONDAY

DATE:

Top three priorities

1...

2...

3...

Any challenges I might face

....

....

....

....

....

....

How I'll overcome them

....

....

....

....

....

....

....

....

 How do I feel this morning?

SCHEDULE:

 Morning ....

....

....

....

....

....

 Afternoon ....

....

....

....

....

 Evening

....

....

....

....

END OF DAY CHECK-IN

What am I proud of achieving today?

What are the biggest lessons I have learnt today?

Three things or people I am grateful for today

How do I feel this evening?

TUESDAY

DATE:

Top three priorities

1. ....

2. ....

3. ....

Any challenges I might face

....

....

....

....

....

....

How I'll overcome them

....

....

....

....

....

....

....

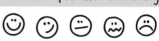

How do I feel this morning?

SCHEDULE:

☀ Morning

....

....

....

....

....

☀ Afternoon

....

....

....

....

....

☽ Evening

....

....

....

....

END OF DAY CHECK-IN

What am I proud of achieving today?

What are the biggest lessons I have learnt today?

Three things or people I am grateful for today

How do I feel this evening?

WEDNESDAY

DATE:

Top three priorities

1...

2...

3...

Any challenges I might face

....

....

....

....

....

....

How I'll overcome them

....

....

....

....

....

....

....

....

How do I feel this morning?

SCHEDULE:

☼ Morning

....

....

....

....

....

☼ Afternoon ....

....

....

....

....

☾ Evening ....

....

....

....

END OF DAY CHECK-IN

What am I proud of achieving today?

What are the biggest lessons I have learnt today?

Three things or people I am grateful for today

How do I feel this evening?

THURSDAY

DATE:

Top three priorities

1. ....

2. ....

3. ....

Any challenges I might face

....

....

....

....

....

....

How I'll overcome them

....

....

....

....

....

....

....

How do I feel this morning?

SCHEDULE:

☀ Morning ....

....

....

....

....

....

☀ Afternoon ....

....

....

....

....

☾ Evening ....

....

....

....

....

END OF DAY CHECK-IN

What am I proud of achieving today?

What are the biggest lessons I have learnt today?

Three things or people I am grateful for today

How do I feel this evening?

FRIDAY

DATE:
....

Top three priorities

1. ....

2. ....

3. ....

Any challenges I might face

....

....

....

....

....

How I'll overcome them

....

....

....

....

....

....

....

How do I feel this morning?

☺ ☺ 😐 😵 ☹

SCHEDULE:

☀ Morning ....

....

....

....

....

....

☀ Afternoon ....

....

....

....

....

☾ Evening ....

....

....

....

END OF DAY CHECK-IN

What am I proud of achieving today?

What are the biggest lessons I have learnt today?

Three things or people I am grateful for today

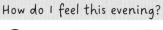
How do I feel this evening?

SATURDAY

DATE:

Top three priorities

1. ....

2. ....

3. ....

Any challenges I might face

....

....

....

....

....

How I'll overcome them

....

....

....

....

....

....

....

How do I feel this morning?

SCHEDULE:

 Morning ....

....

....

....

....

☀ Afternoon ....

....

....

....

....

🌙 Evening ....

....

....

....

END OF DAY CHECK-IN

What am I proud of achieving today?

What are the biggest lessons I have learnt today?

Three things or people I am grateful for today

How do I feel this evening?

SUNDAY

DATE:

Top three priorities

1. ....

2. ....

3. ....

Any challenges I might face

....

....

....

....

....

....

How I'll overcome them

....

....

....

....

....

....

....

....

....

How do I feel this morning?

☺ ☺ 😐 😵 ☹

SCHEDULE:

☀ Morning ....

....

....

....

....

....

☀ Afternoon ....

....

....

....

....

....

☾ Evening ....

....

....

....

....

END OF DAY CHECK-IN

What am I proud of achieving today?

What are the biggest lessons I have learnt today?

Three things or people I am grateful for today

How do I feel this evening?

BRAIN DUMPING PAGE

DATE:

SORT YOUR BRAIN DUMP INTO CATEGORIES

Fill in your categories, then move everything from the main brain dump list into its category.

Category:

Category:

Category:

Category:

Category:

Category:

MONDAY

DATE:

Top three priorities

1. ....

2. ....

3. ....

Any challenges I might face

....

....

....

....

....

How I'll overcome them

....

....

....

....

....

....

....

....

How do I feel this morning?

☺ ☺ 😐 😵 ☹

SCHEDULE:

Morning ....

....

....

....

....

Afternoon ....

....

....

....

....

Evening ....

....

....

....

....

END OF DAY CHECK-IN

What am I proud of achieving today?

What are the biggest lessons I have learnt today?

Three things or people I am grateful for today

How do I feel this evening?

TUESDAY

DATE:

Top three priorities

1. ....

2. ....

3. ....

Any challenges I might face

....

....

....

....

....

....

How I'll overcome them

....

....

....

....

....

....

....

....

How do I feel this morning?

☺ ☺ 😐 😵 ☹

SCHEDULE:

Morning ....

....

....

....

....

....

Afternoon ....

....

....

....

....

Evening ....

....

....

....

END OF DAY CHECK-IN

What am I proud of achieving today?

What are the biggest lessons I have learnt today?

Three things or people I am grateful for today

How do I feel this evening?

WEDNESDAY

DATE:

Top three priorities

1. ....

2. ....

3. ....

Any challenges I might face

....

....

....

....

....

How I'll overcome them

....

....

....

....

....

....

....

How do I feel this morning?

SCHEDULE:

Morning ....

....

....

....

....

Afternoon ....

....

....

....

....

Evening ....

....

....

....

END OF DAY CHECK-IN

What am I proud of achieving today?

What are the biggest lessons I have learnt today?

Three things or people I am grateful for today

How do I feel this evening?

THURSDAY

DATE:

Top three priorities

1...

2...

3...

Any challenges I might face

....

....

....

....

....

....

How I'll overcome them

....

....

....

....

....

....

....

How do I feel this morning?

☺ ☺ ☺ ☺ ☹

SCHEDULE:

☀ Morning ....

....

....

....

....

....

☀ Afternoon ....

....

....

....

....

☾ Evening ....

....

....

END OF DAY CHECK-IN

What am I proud of achieving today?

What are the biggest lessons I have learnt today?

Three things or people I am grateful for today

How do I feel this evening?

FRIDAY

DATE:

Top three priorities

1. ....

2. ....

3. ....

Any challenges I might face

....

....

....

....

....

....

How I'll overcome them

....

....

....

....

....

....

....

How do I feel this morning?

☺ ☺ 😐 😖 ☹

SCHEDULE:

☀ Morning ....

....

....

....

....

....

☀ Afternoon ....

....

....

....

....

....

☾ Evening ....

....

....

....

....

END OF DAY CHECK-IN

What am I proud of achieving today?

What are the biggest lessons I have learnt today?

Three things or people I am grateful for today

How do I feel this evening?

SATURDAY

DATE:

Top three priorities

1. ....

2. ....

3. ....

Any challenges I might face

....

....

....

....

....

....

How I'll overcome them

....

....

....

....

....

....

....

....

How do I feel this morning?

☺ ☺ 😐 😵 ☹

SCHEDULE:

☀ Morning ....

....

....

....

....

....

....

☀ Afternoon ....

....

....

....

....

....

🌙 Evening ....

....

....

....

....

END OF DAY CHECK-IN

What am I proud of achieving today?

What are the biggest lessons I have learnt today?

Three things or people I am grateful for today

How do I feel this evening?

SUNDAY

DATE:

Top three priorities

1. ....

2. ....

3. ....

Any challenges I might face

....

....

....

....

....

....

How I'll overcome them

....

....

....

....

....

....

....

....

How do I feel this morning?

😃 🙂 😐 😵 ☹️

SCHEDULE:

Morning ....

....

....

....

....

....

Afternoon ....

....

....

....

....

Evening ....

....

....

....

END OF DAY CHECK-IN

What am I proud of achieving today?

What are the biggest lessons I have learnt today?

Three things or people I am grateful for today

How do I feel this evening?

BRAIN DUMPING PAGE

DATE:

SORT YOUR BRAIN DUMP INTO CATEGORIES

Fill in your categories, then move everything from the main brain dump list into its category.

Category:

Category:

Category:

Category:

Category:

Category:

MONDAY

DATE:

Top three priorities

1. ....

2. ....

3. ....

Any challenges I might face

....

....

....

....

....

....

How I'll overcome them

....

....

....

....

....

....

....

....

How do I feel this morning?

😊 🙂 😐 😵 ☹️

SCHEDULE:

🌅 Morning ....

....

....

....

....

☀️ Afternoon ....

....

....

....

....

🌙 Evening ....

....

....

....

END OF DAY CHECK-IN

What am I proud of achieving today?

What are the biggest lessons I have learnt today?

Three things or people I am grateful for today

How do I feel this evening?

TUESDAY

DATE:

Top three priorities

1. ....

2. ....

3. ....

Any challenges I might face

....

....

....

....

....

....

How I'll overcome them

....

....

....

....

....

....

....

How do I feel this morning?

☺ ☺ 😐 😖 ☹

SCHEDULE:

☀ Morning ....

....

....

....

....

....

☀ Afternoon ....

....

....

....

....

🌙 Evening ....

....

....

....

END OF DAY CHECK-IN

What am I proud of achieving today?

What are the biggest lessons I have learnt today?

Three things or people I am grateful for today

How do I feel this evening?

WEDNESDAY

DATE:

Top three priorities

1...

2...

3...

Any challenges I might face

....

....

....

....

....

....

How I'll overcome them

....

....

....

....

....

....

....

....

How do I feel this morning?

☺ ☺ ☺ ☺ ☹

SCHEDULE:

☀ Morning ....

....

....

....

....

☀ Afternoon ....

....

....

....

....

☾ Evening ....

....

....

....

END OF DAY CHECK-IN

What am I proud of achieving today?

What are the biggest lessons I have learnt today?

Three things or people I am grateful for today

How do I feel this evening?

THURSDAY

DATE:

Top three priorities

1. ....

2. ....

3. ....

Any challenges I might face

....

....

....

....

....

....

How I'll overcome them

....

....

....

....

....

....

....

....

How do I feel this morning?

☺ ☺ 😐 😵 ☹

SCHEDULE:

Morning

....

....

....

....

....

....

Afternoon ....

....

....

....

....

....

Evening ....

....

....

....

....

END OF DAY CHECK-IN

What am I proud of achieving today?

What are the biggest lessons I have learnt today?

Three things or people I am grateful for today

How do I feel this evening?

FRIDAY

DATE:

Top three priorities

1. ....

2. ....

3. ....

Any challenges I might face

....

....

....

....

....

....

How I'll overcome them

....

....

....

....

....

....

....

....

How do I feel this morning?

☺ ☺ 😐 😵 ☹

SCHEDULE:

☀ Morning ....

....

....

....

....

....

☀ Afternoon ....

....

....

....

....

....

☾ Evening ....

....

....

....

....

END OF DAY CHECK-IN

What am I proud of achieving today?

What are the biggest lessons I have learnt today?

Three things or people I am grateful for today

How do I feel this evening?

SATURDAY

DATE:

_____

Top three priorities

1...

2...

3...

Any challenges I might face

....

....

....

....

....

How I'll overcome them

....

....

....

....

....

....

....

How do I feel this morning?

☺ ☺ ☺ ☺ ☹

SCHEDULE:

☀ Morning ....

....

....

....

....

☀ Afternoon ....

....

....

....

....

☾ Evening ....

....

....

....

END OF DAY CHECK-IN

What am I proud of achieving today?

What are the biggest lessons I have learnt today?

Three things or people I am grateful for today

How do I feel this evening?

SUNDAY

DATE:

....

Top three priorities

1. ....

2. ....

3. ....

Any challenges I might face

....

....

....

....

....

....

How I'll overcome them

....

....

....

....

....

....

....

....

How do I feel this morning?

☺ ☺ 😐 😵 ☹

SCHEDULE:

☀ Morning ....

....

....

....

....

....

☀ Afternoon ....

....

....

....

....

....

☾ Evening ....

....

....

....

....

END OF DAY CHECK-IN

What am I proud of achieving today?

What are the biggest lessons I have learnt today?

Three things or people I am grateful for today

How do I feel this evening?

BRAIN DUMPING PAGE

DATE:

SORT YOUR BRAIN DUMP INTO CATEGORIES

Fill in your categories and then move everything from the main dump list into its category.

Category:

Category:

Category:

Category:

Category:

Category:

MONDAY

DATE:

Top three priorities

1..

2..

3..

Any challenges I might face

....

....

....

....

....

....

How I'll overcome them

....

....

....

....

....

....

....

....

How do I feel this morning?

☺ ☺ 😐 😵 ☹

SCHEDULE:

☀ Morning ....

....

....

....

....

....

☀ Afternoon ....

....

....

....

....

🌙 Evening ....

....

....

....

....

END OF DAY CHECK-IN

What am I proud of achieving today?

What are the biggest lessons I have learnt today?

Three things or people I am grateful for today

How do I feel this evening?

TUESDAY

DATE:

Top three priorities

1. ....

2. ....

3. ....

Any challenges I might face

....

....

....

....

....

....

How I'll overcome them

....

....

....

....

....

....

....

How do I feel this morning?

☺ ☺ 😐 😖 ☹

SCHEDULE:

☀ Morning ....

....

....

....

....

....

☀ Afternoon ....

....

....

....

....

....

🌙 Evening ....

....

....

....

....

END OF DAY CHECK-IN

What am I proud of achieving today?

What are the biggest lessons I have learnt today?

Three things or people I am grateful for today

How do I feel this evening?

WEDNESDAY

DATE:

Top three priorities

1. ....

2. ....

3. ....

Any challenges I might face

....

....

....

....

....

How I'll overcome them

....

....

....

....

....

....

....

How do I feel this morning?

☺ ☺ 😐 😵 ☹

SCHEDULE:

☼ Morning ....

....

....

....

....

☀ Afternoon ....

....

....

....

....

☾ Evening ....

....

....

....

END OF DAY CHECK-IN

What am I proud of achieving today?

What are the biggest lessons I have learnt today?

Three things or people I am grateful for today

How do I feel this evening?

THURSDAY

DATE:

Top three priorities

1. ....

2. ....

3. ....

Any challenges I might face

....

....

....

....

....

How I'll overcome them

....

....

....

....

....

....

....

How do I feel this morning?

😊 🙂 😐 😵 ☹️

SCHEDULE:

☀ Morning

....

....

....

....

....

....

☀ Afternoon ....

....

....

....

....

☾ Evening ....

....

....

....

END OF DAY CHECK-IN

What am I proud of achieving today?

What are the biggest lessons I have learnt today?

Three things or people I am grateful for today

How do I feel this evening?

FRIDAY

DATE:

Top three priorities

1. ....

2. ....

3. ....

Any challenges I might face

....

....

....

....

....

....

How I'll overcome them

....

....

....

....

....

....

....

How do I feel this morning?

☺ ☺ 😐 😖 ☹

SCHEDULE:

☀ Morning ....

....

....

....

....

☀ Afternoon ....

....

....

....

....

🌙 Evening ....

....

....

....

END OF DAY CHECK-IN

What am I proud of achieving today?

What are the biggest lessons I have learnt today?

Three things or people I am grateful for today

How do I feel this evening?

SATURDAY

DATE:

Top three priorities

1...

2...

3...

Any challenges I might face

....

....

....

....

....

How I'll overcome them

....

....

....

....

....

....

....

How do I feel this morning?

☺ ☺ ☺ ☺ ☹

SCHEDULE:

☼ Morning ....

....

....

....

....

☼ Afternoon ....

....

....

....

....

☾ Evening ....

....

....

....

....

END OF DAY CHECK-IN

What am I proud of achieving today?

What are the biggest lessons I have learnt today?

Three things or people I am grateful for today

How do I feel this evening?

SUNDAY

DATE:
_____

Top three priorities

1...

2...

3...

Any challenges I might face

....

....

....

....

....

....

How I'll overcome them

....

....

....

....

....

....

....

How do I feel this morning?

☺ ☺ 😐 😵 ☹

SCHEDULE:

☀ Morning ....

....

....

....

....

☀ Afternoon ....

....

....

....

....

☾ Evening ....

....

....

....

....

END OF DAY CHECK-IN

What am I proud of achieving today?

What are the biggest lessons I have learnt today?

Three things or people I am grateful for today

How do I feel this evening?

BRAIN DUMPING PAGE

DATE:

SORT YOUR BRAIN DUMP INTO CATEGORIES

Fill in your categories and then move everything from the main dump list into its category.

Category:

Category:

Category:

Category:

Category:

Category:

END OF MONTH CHECK-IN

Start by listing your top five to ten achievements this month

1. ....
2. ....
3. ....
4. ....
5. ....
6. ....
7. ....
8. ....
9. ....
10. ....

Are there any things that didn't go quite so well? Try to approach this gently and without judgement.

YOUR WHEEL OF LIFE

The wheel of life is a great tool for helping you to gain perspective on what areas of your wellbeing are going well and where you might be feeling overwhelmed.

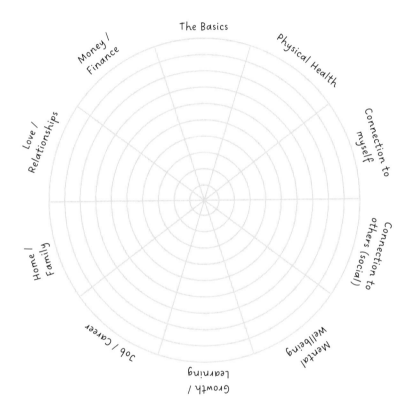

HOW TO USE:

- Visit each section and rate how good you feel about that part of your life (0 is in the middle and the lowest, 10 is the outer edge and the best).

- Draw a line to connect the dots, which will create a new circle – most of the time, a wonky one!

- The new perimeter of the circle represents your wheel of life. Is it a smooth or a bumpy ride? Are there any areas that stand out as needing attention? Perhaps these areas are making you feel particularly overwhelmed? Consider this as you reflect on your month.

CARRYING FORWARD YOUR BRAIN DUMP

Is there anything from your brain dump lists this month you keep putting off? List those tasks here.

Now, spend a moment considering what might be preventing you from completing those tasks. Do they bring up something uncomfortable for you? Do you feel anxious about them? Maybe you're stuck in 'analysis paralysis'. Write down any thoughts or feelings that come up when you think about these unfinished tasks.

Task I'm stuck on	Why it's making me feel stuck

LETTING GO AND MOVING FORWARD

Are there any of the tasks on your list that you need to let go of for any reason? For example, maybe they're just not needed anymore. Maybe they're making you feel more overwhelmed? List them here.

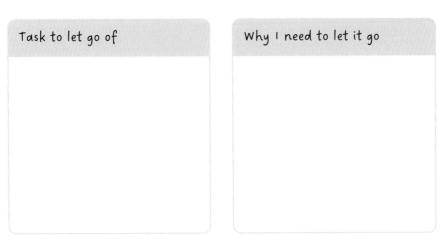

Task to let go of	Why I need to let it go

Are there any tasks on your list that you really want to achieve in the next month? Write them down and prioritise them in your next brain dump!

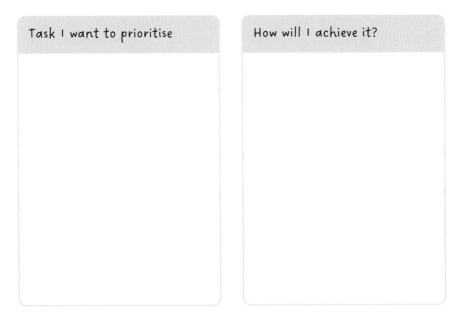

Task I want to prioritise	How will I achieve it?

PART TWO:

Untangling Your Mind

———

Now we know why our minds might feel
overwhelmed, let's start gently untangling
everything that's taking up space.

Hopefully, by now, you've got into the swing of things with your brain dumping pages. Or, if you've skipped ahead to this section, you have a good idea of where to start. In Part Two, we'll look at how we can untangle our minds even further with good routines, planning and decluttering. We'll also dig into some motivational tricks to help when you feel like you just can't get started.

It's really important to note that different things work for different people and so, in this section, I've tried to include various ways you can untangle your mind. This doesn't mean that you need to use absolutely every single technique all at once (and, actually, that might make things more overwhelming). Instead, go through each of the tools and then pick one that makes the most sense for your life. If it works, amazing! You may want to add another one and try that too. If it doesn't stick, don't be afraid to ditch it and try something else.

While you're going through this section, keep going with your regular brain dumping. These tools and techniques are there to complement your brain dumping practice and help make things less overwhelming for you, but the cornerstone really is that weekly dump!

MANAGING YOUR SCHEDULE BY ENERGY LEVELS

So, you've done your weekly brain dump and now you've got 101 tasks that you need to schedule throughout the week (or at least it feels that way). Now, you could schedule them in your planner randomly in the hope that you'll be feeling motivated enough to get them done when the time arises. Or, you can use your natural energy levels to help you stay on top of your schedule. Let me show you how...

EARLY BIRD OR NIGHT OWL?

Let's start by working out when it's best to do certain tasks during your day depending on your circadian rhythm. Your circadian rhythm is like your body's inner clock and it can impact your sleep patterns and energy levels. The two most common types of circadian rhythm are early birds and night owls. Not sure which one you fall into? Answer these questions to help you decide:

· When your alarm goes off in the morning, do you jump out of bed or are you constantly hitting snooze?
· When it gets to mid-afternoon, are you feeling sleepy and done with the day or ready to take on the world?
· Are you ready to crawl into bed as soon as it gets dark or are you still wide awake come midnight (not for any other reason other than your energy levels are high)?

If you're more of a jump out of bed first thing, but ready to sleep by 9pm then you're likely an early bird. However, if you're energy doesn't seem to kick in until the afternoon then you're probably a night owl.

Knowing this can help you understand how to plan and schedule your days better. Your most complex and all-consuming work should be done when energy levels are highest – so first thing for early birds and later in the day for night owls. I'm generally an early bird and knowing this means I can ensure all of my energy-sapping tasks get done first thing – usually within the first few hours of waking up. Anything that doesn't need my full attention gets done in the afternoon and early evening. But what if your energy levels fluctuate throughout the days, weeks and months? This can be common when hormone levels change or when living with chronic conditions that make it more difficult to plan ahead. Well, that's where another one of my favourite tools comes in...

THE ANTI-BURNOUT MATRIX

Whilst I'd generally consider myself an early bird, there are times when I don't want to bounce out of bed and get my 'best work' done first thing. For me, this is generally dictated by hormones, or if I've had a really taxing day the day before and feel drained. I created 'The Anti-Burnout Matrix' to help me plan my days depending on my energy levels and it's now used by many of our members as a gentler, more intuitive way of planning their days.

The matrix is as shown here, and you can download a blank copy from www.davidandcharles.com.

On the left-hand side is your to-do list and on the right is the matrix itself. This is split into four sections depending on high or low mental and physical energy levels. Once you've brain dumped your to-do list, move tasks into the box that best represents what kind of energy they need. For example:

- Household chores may need high physical energy, but low mental energy, so it goes in the top left box.
- Writing this book needs high mental energy but low physical energy for me, so it goes in the bottom right box.
- Meetings or socialising need both high physical and mental energy generally, so they go in the top right box.
- And anything I can do basically on autopilot – generally self-care activities – are the low energy tasks that go in the bottom left box.

Once your to-do list has been moved into the appropriate boxes, check in with yourself throughout the day and see how your energy levels are. Use this to pick a task from the appropriate section and get working on it.

It can take a little while to get used to this and be able to recognise your mental and physical energy levels, but once you've got it down, it can be a huge game-changer.

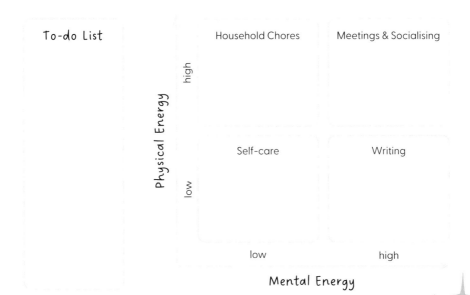

You may also be able to recognise patterns that will make it easier to schedule your time going forward. For example, I know that there are certain times in my day that work best for meetings and the rest of my calendar gets blocked for other types of work. I also know that I need really low-energy tasks around the afternoon slump so don't schedule in anything too taxing here.

Scheduling your life around your energy levels can make a huge difference to how much you can actually tick off your list every day. We all have natural peaks and troughs, so instead of getting frustrated when the afternoon slump kicks in, consider how you can make it work for you.

MORNING AND
EVENING ROUTINES

One of the best cures for overwhelm is routine and habit, but I know that's often easier said than done! We're bombarded by images and videos of the 'perfect' morning routines on social media, and that can make us feel as though we're getting it all wrong. But realistically, most people don't have time for an hour at the gym, an hour of self-development reading and a gallon of green juice before they start their day.

Remember, comparisonitis can make us feel more overwhelmed, and many of the people who film these videos do this as a full-time job. I've yet to see someone have that morning routine and then have to wrestle their kids into the car for school before heading to a 12-hour shift at a busy hospital emergency department.

When it comes to creating new routines, these have to be realistic and work for you. The best place to start is by looking at what you already do on autopilot. Perhaps your morning routine looks something like this:

- Wake-up in a daze after snoozing the alarm several times
- 3-minute bathroom break

- 10 minutes to shower and get ready
- 5 minutes to quickly wolf something down for breakfast
- Get the rest of the house ready
- Head out the door

This schedule makes me feel overwhelmed just looking at it, and if we start our day feeling overwhelmed then it's a feeling that can be carried forward throughout the rest of the day. The key to making it less overwhelming is to add some overwhelm-busters to the things you do already on autopilot. I'll go through different self-care tools to help reduce overwhelm in Part Three, but let's take a look at how we can make this morning routine a little less hectic.

- *Wake-up without hitting the snooze.* Try a sunrise alarm or move your alarm clock out of reach so you have to get up and turn it off.
- *Drink a huge glass of water before anything else.* It's the world's best natural energy drink and can help your mind feel clearer when you wake up.
- *Make your bed.* Give yourself an early dopamine rush by ticking one thing off your to-do list as soon as you get out of bed.
- *Use your bathroom break to go through the to-do list you made the night before.* Make sorting out your to-do list part of your evening routine, then you'll only need to review it in the morning. It's a lot less overwhelming just to remind yourself what you have to do that day, rather than trying to plan out the day first thing.
- *Have a mindful shower.* Use all of your senses to enjoy that 10 minutes to yourself, and give your mind a little reset.
- *Enjoy a kitchen disco whilst making breakfast or getting the morning chores done.* Getting active can help boost endorphins and, again, make our minds feel clearer.

This routine shouldn't take longer than the one outlined before it. The only difference is, we're stacking some overwhelm-busters on top of what we already do. Sure, there will be times when some of this is impossible (if someone bangs on the bathroom door during your mindful shower), but even one morning a week like this will help you feel less overwhelmed.

Consider your evening routine too. What does that look like? Is there anything you can do the night before that will help make things easier in the morning? Here are some ideas for things you can add to your evening routine:

- *Sort your to-do list for the next day.* Before you go to bed, make life easier for 'tomorrow you' by jotting down your priorities and appointment reminders. This can also really help with any bedtime anxiety that might come from having too much on your mind to remember.
- *Prep anything you can.* Whether that's scraping leftovers into a lunchbox for tomorrow, or having all your clothes ready for the morning, the more you can do the night before, the better.
- *Reduce phone usage before bed.* I'm guilty of a late-night social media scroll as much as anyone, but I really notice the negative effects the next day. Where possible, put your phone away at least 30 minutes before bed for better sleep and less nighttime comparisonitis.
- *Journal and reflect.* Help clear your mind and practise gratitude with your end of day check-in page. It can help you sleep more soundly if you celebrate what went right that day, before you go to sleep.

These are just examples and your evening routine might look even more hectic than your morning one, depending on your working hours, household, and so on. However, as with the morning routine, look at what you do on autopilot already and see if there's anything that can be added in without too much disruption.

One important note about habits and routines – don't try and change everything all at once! I say it often, but making drastic, overnight change is a one-way ticket to overwhelm. Instead, pick one new habit you'd like to add to your routine and let your brain get used to that change before adding in anything new.

DECLUTTERING YOUR SPACE AND MIND

While it may be a cliché, there's truth in the saying, 'tidy home, tidy mind". When we feel as though our space is cluttered and messy, it can really add to the clutter and noise in our minds. August Gawen, a minimalist expert, once explained it best to me when they said it's like a 'silent to-do list'. When you move through your home or workspace, are there things crying out to you 'clean me, fix me, water me, deal with me'?

Chances are, even if you're not conscious of clutter having an impact on your overwhelm, it will have. That being said, when we're already overwhelmed, the thought of trying to declutter anything may only add to that feeling. It's a catch-22 situation – wanting to declutter to help with the overwhelm, but being too overwhelmed to start. Here are some tips offered by the experts during our previous 'Mindful Minimalism' theme at The Anti-Burnout Club:

- *Break the decluttering down into small, manageable chunks.* Even if that means focusing on one small area, like a chest of drawers or cupboard, to begin with.
- *Order your tasks in a way that makes you feel good.* Start off with quick wins that will make you feel a sense of accomplishment, and get those done. Then move on to bigger jobs and projects.
- *Stay in one place and sort items into piles around you.* Instead of putting each item away as you find it, keep your focus in one place so you don't end up trying to tackle too many different areas at once, or getting distracted.

- *Get it out of the house!* Instead of bagging up everything and then moving those bags or boxes around the house, promise yourself you'll get it out ASAP. That means taking clothes straight to the charity shop, or rubbish down to the tip, so it doesn't create more clutter.

- *Use it or lose it.* The easiest way to ditch the clutter is to get rid of anything you don't use or will have no future use for. As you go through the decluttering process be honest with yourself – if you don't use it, lose it! Avoid holding on to items 'just in case'. You may also want to see if items light you up or if you truly love them (Marie Kondo style) when decluttering.

- *Cash in your clutter.* Use sites like eBay, Vinted or Facebook Marketplace to sell items you no longer need but are too good to throw away. This serves a double purpose of getting it out of the house and making you a little bit of spare cash.

- *Just remember that it's going to look worse before it gets better!* Normally when we get to the halfway point it can feel overwhelming – use the motivation tips below to help you get it over the finish line.

Even if you spend just 5-10 minutes decluttering a day, it all adds up. Once you've completed your first big declutter, you're likely to find it easier to keep on top of too. When you're done with an area, consider how doing this made you feel. Do you feel lighter? Calmer? More at ease? Remember that feeling and use it to carry you through your next declutter!

FROM TO-DO TO DONE: GETTING MOTIVATED

If you're anything like me, then the planning aspect of all of this can feel quite easy. You may have dumped everything out and know exactly what you need to do, or set your new routine up ready for a less overwhelming day, but then it comes to actually doing it and... well, that's the hard part isn't it? Let's look at some of the tools I use to get motivated and make sure that 'to-do' list actually becomes a 'done' list.

2-MINUTE TRICK

The hardest part about getting motivated is just getting started. This little trick can help get the ball rolling without adding to the overwhelm.

First, pick something off your to-do list you'd like to get done but feel some kind of resistance to. I call these the 'Big Scary Tasks'. Now, set a timer for 2 minutes and promise yourself you'll work on it for just 2 minutes. That's it!

Generally, we can promise ourselves that we will do 2 minutes of practically anything. It doesn't feel so daunting when it's just a couple of minutes. What tends to happen is that when we get started we then feel as though we could probably do another 2 minutes, and then another, and so on. Once you've got the ball rolling, it's much easier to keep the momentum going. However, getting over that initial hurdle is where most of the resistance will come from. Give it a try with something you've been putting off, and see how you get on.

POMODORO TECHNIQUE

Another great tool that involves a timer is the 'pomodoro technique', which I've used almost daily for around ten years. In fact, I'm using it to write this right now! First, pick a task you want to give your full attention and focus, whether it's a work project, housework, or something else.

Now, set a timer for 25 minutes and make sure that there is nothing that can distract you in that 25-minute period. You can find certain apps to block distractions on your phone or computer for this.

Once your 25 minutes of focus is up, set a 5-minute timer for your break period. Use this time to reset and fit in some form of self-care if possible. Grab a glass of water, have a stretch, whatever works for you.

Repeat this cycle four times (for a total of 2 hours) before having a longer break or until you've completed the task(s). You may want to adapt the cycle lengths to better suit your day, but the reason this works so well is because 25 minutes is about how long our brains can focus before they get distracted. Fitting in a 5-minute break to reset can actually help you feel more motivated and productive in the long run.

THE PAIRING TRICK

This is a really simple technique but one that can be really effective if you put it to good use. All you have to do is pair any tasks you don't want to do with something you really enjoy doing. For example:

· Tidying the house whilst listening to your favourite podcast
· Doing any form of exercise or movement in front of your favourite show
· Putting together an epic playlist of your favourite songs to listen to when working

The trick to really making this work, however, is to only do that thing you love whilst you're doing the thing you don't want to do. So, you can only listen to your favourite podcast whilst you're decluttering the house. If you're desperate to watch the next episode of a binge-worthy Netflix drama, but can only do so whilst you're ticking things off the to-do list, imagine how much you'll get done!

Of course, this won't work for absolutely everything, but try pairing some of your mundane, autopilot tasks with something more fun to get them ticked off the list.

BREAK IT DOWN FURTHER

Sometimes we can feel unmotivated and overwhelmed by a huge task that's looming over us. If we look at it as one insurmountable mountain of a task, it might feel impossible to get started. In this case, we may need to go back to our brain dump and break things down even further.

Let's take this book as an example. When I thought about writing the entire thing as a whole project, I felt seriously overwhelmed. And no, the irony of that situation was not lost on me! In order for me to scale this mountain, I had to break it down into smaller, more manageable tasks. For me, that meant every section within every chapter had to have its own 'to-do'.

Think about projects in your life that seem overwhelming because of their size. Maybe it's decluttering the whole house, writing an entire essay, or getting a work presentation done on time. Now think about how you can break this down into smaller, more manageable chunks. Even if they seem tiny and insignificant, write each task down.

What happens is that it becomes much easier to finish those smaller tasks off and, each time we do, we get a lovely dopamine rush from ticking something off the list. This helps us feel more motivated and less overwhelmed, compared to looking it at as one big daunting task.

The next time you brain dump and there's a larger project on the list, see if you can break it down into much smaller milestones before adding those into your schedule. Remember to tick off each task as you go to help boost motivation.

PICTURE THE END

When I'm really struggling to get anything done, I like to imagine how I'll feel when I've ticked that thing off the list. This is particularly helpful for those 'Big Scary Tasks' that I've been putting off for one reason or another.

Close your eyes and bring to mind what the finish line looks like. How do you feel now you've completed whatever task it is you're struggling with? Do you feel happy? Relieved? Accomplished? Really imagine that you're experiencing that feeling of completing the task you're putting off. It feels good, right?

Compare it to how you're feeling right now – probably full of guilt and negative self-talk for not being able to get it done – and use that to spur you on. Keep telling yourself, 'I'm going to feel so proud of myself', 'I'll be so relieved and much calmer when I've ticked this off', 'I'm excited about getting it done'. It's far more motivating than the 'I'm useless for not getting this done' inner monologue we're often faced with when we can't seem to complete something.

You've now got lots of new tools that I hope will help further your brain dumping and also help you tick things off the list. Remember, pick just one to start with, and make sure you feel happy with it fitting into your life before adding new ones. Keep it simple and don't overwhelm yourself with too many changes at once.

In the final section, we'll look at some self-care techniques you can use to help reduce overwhelm even further. We'll also round up with some final tips and my biggest takeaway from my own experiences with overcoming overwhelm.

NOTES

BIG BRAIN DUMP
PART TWO

DATE:

SORT YOUR BRAIN DUMP INTO CATEGORIES

Fill in your categories and then move everything from the main dump list into its category.

Category:

Category:

Category:

Category:

Category:

Category:

Everything else:

MONDAY

DATE:

Top three priorities

1...

2...

3...

Any challenges I might face

....

....

....

....

....

....

How I'll overcome them

....

....

....

....

....

....

....

....

How do I feel this morning?

😃 🙂 😐 😵 ☹️

SCHEDULE:

☀ Morning ....

....

....

....

....

....

☀ Afternoon ....

....

....

....

....

☾ Evening ....

....

....

....

END OF DAY CHECK-IN

What am I proud of achieving today?

What are the biggest lessons I have learnt today?

Three things or people I am grateful for today

How do I feel this evening?

TUESDAY

DATE:

Top three priorities

1. ....

2. ....

3. ....

Any challenges I might face

....

....

....

....

....

....

How I'll overcome them

....

....

....

....

....

....

....

....

How do I feel this morning?

☺ ☺ 😐 😖 ☹

SCHEDULE:

Morning ....

....

....

....

....

Afternoon ....

....

....

....

....

Evening ....

....

....

....

END OF DAY CHECK-IN

What am I proud of achieving today?

What are the biggest lessons I have learnt today?

Three things or people I am grateful for today

How do I feel this evening?

WEDNESDAY

DATE:

Top three priorities

1. ....

2. ....

3. ....

Any challenges I might face

....

....

....

....

....

....

How I'll overcome them

....

....

....

....

....

....

....

How do I feel this morning?

SCHEDULE:

Morning ....

....

....

....

....

Afternoon ....

....

....

....

....

Evening ....

....

....

....

....

END OF DAY CHECK-IN

What am I proud of achieving today?

What are the biggest lessons I have learnt today?

Three things or people I am grateful for today

How do I feel this evening?

THURSDAY

DATE:

Top three priorities

1...

2...

3...

Any challenges I might face

....
....
....
....
....

How I'll overcome them

....
....
....
....
....
....
....
....

How do I feel this morning?

SCHEDULE:

Morning ....
....
....
....
....

Afternoon ....
....
....
....
....

Evening ....
....
....
....

END OF DAY CHECK-IN

What am I proud of achieving today?

What are the biggest lessons I have learnt today?

Three things or people I am grateful for today

How do I feel this evening?

FRIDAY

DATE:

Top three priorities

1...

2...

3...

Any challenges I might face

....

....

....

....

....

....

How I'll overcome them

....

....

....

....

....

....

....

....

How do I feel this morning?

☺ ☺ 😐 😵 ☹

SCHEDULE:

☀ Morning ....

....

....

....

....

☀ Afternoon ....

....

....

....

....

☾ Evening ....

....

....

....

END OF DAY CHECK-IN

What am I proud of achieving today?

What are the biggest lessons I have learnt today?

Three things or people I am grateful for today

How do I feel this evening?

SATURDAY

DATE:

Top three priorities

1...

2...

3...

Any challenges I might face

....

....

....

....

....

....

How I'll overcome them

....

....

....

....

....

....

....

....

How do I feel this morning?

☺ ☺ 😐 🥴 ☹

SCHEDULE:

☀ Morning ....

....

....

....

....

☀ Afternoon ....

....

....

....

....

🌙 Evening ....

....

....

....

END OF DAY CHECK-IN

What am I proud of achieving today?

What are the biggest lessons I have learnt today?

Three things or people I am grateful for today

How do I feel this evening?

SUNDAY

DATE:

Top three priorities

1. ....

2. ....

3. ....

Any challenges I might face

....

....

....

....

....

How I'll overcome them

....

....

....

....

....

....

....

....

How do I feel this morning?

☺ ☺ 😐 😵 ☹

SCHEDULE:

☀ Morning ....

....

....

....

....

....

☀ Afternoon ....

....

....

....

....

🌙 Evening ....

....

....

....

END OF DAY CHECK-IN

What am I proud of achieving today?

What are the biggest lessons I have learnt today?

Three things or people I am grateful for today

How do I feel this evening?

BRAIN DUMPING PAGE

DATE:

SORT YOUR BRAIN DUMP INTO CATEGORIES

Fill in your categories and then move everything from the main dump list into its category.

Category:

Category:

Category:

Category:

Category:

Category:

MONDAY

DATE:

Top three priorities

1. ....

2. ....

3. ....

Any challenges I might face

....

....

....

....

....

....

How I'll overcome them

....

....

....

....

....

....

How do I feel this morning?

😊 🙂 😐 😖 ☹️

SCHEDULE:

🌅 Morning ....

....

....

....

....

....

☀️ Afternoon ....

....

....

....

....

🌙 Evening ....

....

....

....

END OF DAY CHECK-IN

What am I proud of achieving today?

What are the biggest lessons I have learnt today?

Three things or people I am grateful for today

How do I feel this evening?

TUESDAY

DATE:

Top three priorities

1. ....

2. ....

3. ....

Any challenges I might face

....

....

....

....

....

....

How I'll overcome them

....

....

....

....

....

....

....

....

How do I feel this morning?

☺ ☺ 😐 😵 ☹

SCHEDULE:

🌅 Morning ....

....

....

....

....

....

☀️ Afternoon ....

....

....

....

....

....

🌙 Evening ....

....

....

....

....

END OF DAY CHECK-IN

What am I proud of achieving today?

What are the biggest lessons I have learnt today?

Three things or people I am grateful for today

How do I feel this evening?

WEDNESDAY

DATE:

Top three priorities

1. ....

2. ....

3. ....

Any challenges I might face

....

....

....

....

....

....

How I'll overcome them

....

....

....

....

....

....

....

....

How do I feel this morning?

☺ ☺ 😐 😖 ☹

SCHEDULE:

☀ Morning ....

....

....

....

....

☀ Afternoon ....

....

....

....

....

☾ Evening ....

....

....

....

....

END OF DAY CHECK-IN

What am I proud of achieving today?

What are the biggest lessons I have learnt today?

Three things or people I am grateful for today

How do I feel this evening?

THURSDAY

DATE:

Top three priorities

1. ....

2. ....

3. ....

Any challenges I might face

....

....

....

....

....

....

How I'll overcome them

....

....

....

....

....

....

....

....

How do I feel this morning?

☺ ☺ 😐 😵 ☹

SCHEDULE:

☀ Morning ....

....

....

....

....

....

☀ Afternoon ....

....

....

....

....

....

🌙 Evening ....

....

....

....

....

END OF DAY CHECK-IN

What am I proud of achieving today?

What are the biggest lessons I have learnt today?

Three things or people I am grateful for today

How do I feel this evening?

FRIDAY

DATE:

Top three priorities

1. ....

2. ....

3. ....

Any challenges I might face

....

....

....

....

....

....

How I'll overcome them

....

....

....

....

....

....

....

....

How do I feel this morning?

☺ ☺ 😐 😵 ☹

SCHEDULE:

🌅 Morning ....

....

....

....

....

....

☀ Afternoon ....

....

....

....

....

🌙 Evening ....

....

....

END OF DAY CHECK-IN

What am I proud of achieving today?

What are the biggest lessons I have learnt today?

Three things or people I am grateful for today

How do I feel this evening?

SATURDAY

DATE:

Top three priorities

1...

2...

3...

Any challenges I might face

....

....

....

....

....

....

How I'll overcome them

....

....

....

....

....

....

....

....

How do I feel this morning?

☺ 🙂 😐 😖 ☹

SCHEDULE:

☀ Morning ....

....

....

....

....

....

☀ Afternoon ....

....

....

....

....

....

☾ Evening ....

....

....

....

END OF DAY CHECK-IN

What am I proud of achieving today?

What are the biggest lessons I have learnt today?

Three things or people I am grateful for today

How do I feel this evening?

SUNDAY

DATE:

Top three priorities

1. ....

2. ....

3. ....

Any challenges I might face

....
....
....
....
....
....

How I'll overcome them

....
....
....
....
....
....
....
....

How do I feel this morning?

☺ ☺ 😐 😵 ☹

SCHEDULE:

☀ Morning ....
....
....
....
....
....

☀ Afternoon ....
....
....
....
....

☽ Evening ....
....
....
....

END OF DAY CHECK-IN

What am I proud of achieving today?

What are the biggest lessons I have learnt today?

Three things or people I am grateful for today

How do I feel this evening?

BRAIN DUMPING PAGE

SORT YOUR BRAIN DUMP INTO CATEGORIES

Fill in your categories and then move everything from the main dump list into its category.

Category:

Category:

Category:

Category:

Category:

Category:

MONDAY

DATE:

_____

Top three priorities

1. ....

2. ....

3. ....

Any challenges I might face

....
....
....
....
....
....

How I'll overcome them

....
....
....
....
....
....
....
....

How do I feel this morning?

☺ ☺ 😐 😵 ☹

SCHEDULE:

☀ Morning ....
....
....
....
....
....

☀ Afternoon ....
....
....
....
....

🌙 Evening ....
....
....
....
....

END OF DAY CHECK-IN

What am I proud of achieving today?

What are the biggest lessons I have learnt today?

Three things or people I am grateful for today

How do I feel this evening?

TUESDAY

DATE:

Top three priorities

1. ....

2. ....

3. ....

Any challenges I might face

....

....

....

....

....

....

How I'll overcome them

....

....

....

....

....

....

....

....

How do I feel this morning?

SCHEDULE:

☀ Morning ....

....

....

....

....

....

☼ Afternoon ....

....

....

....

....

☾ Evening ....

....

....

....

END OF DAY CHECK-IN

What am I proud of achieving today?

What are the biggest lessons I have learnt today?

Three things or people I am grateful for today

How do I feel this evening?

WEDNESDAY

DATE:

Top three priorities

1. ....

2. ....

3. ....

Any challenges I might face

....

....

....

....

....

....

How I'll overcome them

....

....

....

....

....

....

....

....

How do I feel this morning?

☺ ☺ 😐 😵 ☹

SCHEDULE:

Morning ....

....

....

....

....

Afternoon ....

....

....

....

....

Evening ....

....

....

....

END OF DAY CHECK-IN

What am I proud of achieving today?

What are the biggest lessons I have learnt today?

Three things or people I am grateful for today

How do I feel this evening?

THURSDAY

DATE:

Top three priorities

1...

2...

3...

Any challenges I might face

....

....

....

....

....

....

How I'll overcome them

....

....

....

....

....

....

....

....

How do I feel this morning?

☺ ☺ 😐 😵 ☹

SCHEDULE:

☀ Morning ....

....

....

....

....

....

☀ Afternoon ....

....

....

....

....

☾ Evening ....

....

....

....

END OF DAY CHECK-IN

What am I proud of achieving today?

What are the biggest lessons I have learnt today?

Three things or people I am grateful for today

How do I feel this evening?

FRIDAY

DATE:

Top three priorities

1. ....

2. ....

3. ....

Any challenges I might face

....

....

....

....

....

....

How I'll overcome them

....

....

....

....

....

....

....

How do I feel this morning?

☺ ☺ 😐 😵 ☹

SCHEDULE:

☀ Morning ....

....

....

....

....

....

☀ Afternoon ....

....

....

....

....

☾ Evening ....

....

....

....

....

END OF DAY CHECK-IN

What am I proud of achieving today?

What are the biggest lessons I have learnt today?

Three things or people I am grateful for today

How do I feel this evening?

SATURDAY

DATE:

Top three priorities

1. ....

2. ....

3. ....

Any challenges I might face

....

....

....

....

....

....

How I'll overcome them

....

....

....

....

....

....

....

How do I feel this morning?

☺ ☺ 😐 😵 ☹

SCHEDULE:

Morning ....

....

....

....

....

....

Afternoon ....

....

....

....

....

Evening ....

....

....

....

END OF DAY CHECK-IN

What am I proud of achieving today?

What are the biggest lessons I have learnt today?

Three things or people I am grateful for today

How do I feel this evening?

SUNDAY

DATE:

Top three priorities

1. ....

2. ....

3. ....

Any challenges I might face

....

....

....

....

....

How I'll overcome them

....

....

....

....

....

....

....

How do I feel this morning?

☺ ☺ 😐 😵 ☹

SCHEDULE:

☀ Morning ....

....

....

....

....

....

☀ Afternoon ....

....

....

....

☾ Evening ....

....

....

....

END OF DAY CHECK-IN

What am I proud of achieving today?

What are the biggest lessons I have learnt today?

Three things or people I am grateful for today

How do I feel this evening?

BRAIN DUMPING PAGE

DATE:

SORT YOUR BRAIN DUMP INTO CATEGORIES

Fill in your categories and then move everything from the main dump list into its category.

Category:

Category:

Category:

Category:

Category:

Category:

MONDAY

DATE:

Top three priorities

1. ....

2. ....

3. ....

Any challenges I might face

....

....

....

....

....

....

How I'll overcome them

....

....

....

....

....

....

....

How do I feel this morning?

☺ ☺ 😐 😵 ☹

SCHEDULE:

☀ Morning ....

....

....

....

....

☀ Afternoon ....

....

....

....

....

🌙 Evening ....

....

....

....

END OF DAY CHECK-IN

What am I proud of achieving today?

What are the biggest lessons I have learnt today?

Three things or people I am grateful for today

How do I feel this evening?

TUESDAY

DATE:

Top three priorities

1. ....

2. ....

3. ....

Any challenges I might face

....

....

....

....

....

....

How I'll overcome them

....

....

....

....

....

....

....

How do I feel this morning?

😊 🙂 😐 😵 ☹️

SCHEDULE:

☀ Morning ....

....

....

....

....

....

☀ Afternoon ....

....

....

....

....

....

🌙 Evening ....

....

....

....

....

END OF DAY CHECK-IN

What am I proud of achieving today?

What are the biggest lessons I have learnt today?

Three things or people I am grateful for today

How do I feel this evening?

WEDNESDAY

DATE:

Top three priorities

1. ....

2. ....

3. ....

Any challenges I might face

....

....

....

....

....

How I'll overcome them

....

....

....

....

....

....

....

How do I feel this morning?

☺ ☺ ☺ ☺ ☹

SCHEDULE:

☀ Morning ....

....

....

....

....

....

☀ Afternoon ....

....

....

....

....

☽ Evening ....

....

....

....

END OF DAY CHECK-IN

What am I proud of achieving today?

What are the biggest lessons I have learnt today?

Three things or people I am grateful for today

How do I feel this evening?

THURSDAY

DATE:

Top three priorities

1. ....

2. ....

3. ....

Any challenges I might face

....

....

....

....

....

How I'll overcome them

....

....

....

....

....

....

....

How do I feel this morning?

☺ ☺ 😐 😖 ☹

SCHEDULE:

☀ Morning ....

....

....

....

....

☀ Afternoon ....

....

....

....

....

☾ Evening ....

....

....

....

....

END OF DAY CHECK-IN

What am I proud of achieving today?

What are the biggest lessons I have learnt today?

Three things or people I am grateful for today

How do I feel this evening?

FRIDAY

DATE:

Top three priorities

1. ....

2. ....

3. ....

Any challenges I might face

....

....

....

....

....

How I'll overcome them

....

....

....

....

....

....

....

How do I feel this morning?

☺ ☺ 😐 😖 ☹

SCHEDULE:

☀ Morning ....

....

....

....

☀ Afternoon ....

....

....

....

☽ Evening ....

....

....

....

END OF DAY CHECK-IN

What am I proud of achieving today?

What are the biggest lessons I have learnt today?

Three things or people I am grateful for today

How do I feel this evening?

SATURDAY

DATE:

Top three priorities

1. ....

2. ....

3. ....

Any challenges I might face

....

....

....

....

....

....

How I'll overcome them

....

....

....

....

....

....

....

How do I feel this morning?

☺ ☺ 😐 😵 ☹

SCHEDULE:

Morning ....

....

....

....

....

Afternoon ....

....

....

....

Evening ....

....

....

....

END OF DAY CHECK-IN

What am I proud of achieving today?

What are the biggest lessons I have learnt today?

Three things or people I am grateful for today

How do I feel this evening?

SUNDAY

DATE:

Top three priorities

1. ....

2. ....

3. ....

Any challenges I might face

....

....

....

....

....

....

How I'll overcome them

....

....

....

....

....

....

....

....

How do I feel this morning?

SCHEDULE:

Morning ....

....

....

....

....

Afternoon ....

....

....

....

....

Evening ....

....

....

....

END OF DAY CHECK-IN

What am I proud of achieving today?

What are the biggest lessons I have learnt today?

Three things or people I am grateful for today

How do I feel this evening?

BRAIN DUMPING PAGE

DATE:

SORT YOUR BRAIN DUMP INTO CATEGORIES

Fill in your categories and then move everything from the main dump list into its category.

Category:

Category:

Category:

Category:

Category:

Category:

END OF MONTH CHECK-IN

Start by listing your top five to ten achievements this month

1. ....
2. ....
3. ....
4. ....
5. ....
6. ....
7. ....
8. ....
9. ....
10. ....

Are there any things that didn't go quite so well? Try to approach this gently and without judgement.

YOUR WHEEL OF LIFE

The wheel of life is a great tool for helping you to gain perspective on what areas of your wellbeing are going well and where you might be feeling overwhelmed.

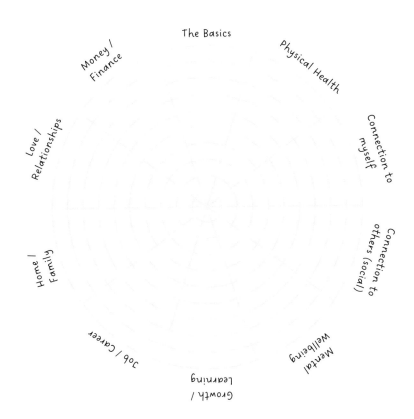

HOW TO USE:

- Visit each section and rate how good you feel about that part of your life (0 is in the middle and the lowest, 10 is the outer edge and the best).
- Draw a line to connect the dots, which will create a new circle – most of the time, a wonky one!
- The new perimeter of the circle represents your wheel of life. Is it a smooth or a bumpy ride? Are there any areas that stand out as needing attention? Perhaps these areas are making you feel particularly overwhelmed? Consider this as you reflect on your month.

CARRYING FORWARD YOUR BRAIN DUMP

Is there anything from your brain dump lists this month you keep putting off? List those tasks here.

Now, spend a moment considering what might be preventing you from completing those tasks. Do they bring up something uncomfortable for you? Do you feel anxious about them? Maybe you're stuck in 'analysis paralysis'. Write down any thoughts or feelings that come up when you think about these unfinished tasks.

Task I'm stuck on	Why it's making me feel stuck

LETTING GO AND MOVING FORWARD

Are there any of the tasks on your list that you need to let go of for any reason? For example, maybe they're just not needed anymore. Maybe they're making you feel more overwhelmed? List them here.

Task to let go of	Why I need to let it go

Are there any tasks on your list that you really want to achieve in the next month? Write them down and prioritise them in your next brain dump!

Task I want to prioritise	How will I achieve it?

PART THREE:

Techniques to Reduce Overwhelm For Good (Almost)

───────

Let's round off this journey with even more ways we can overcome overwhelm, from boundaries to yoga.

You've made it to the final part of this overcoming overwhelm journey. Congratulations! I know how hard it can be to find 10 minutes to yourself to read when you're already feeling overwhelmed, so you should be extremely proud of yourself for getting this far.

In this last section, we're going to look at some techniques that can be incorporated into daily life to reduce overwhelm even further. Now, it's important to note that we are never likely to be rid of overwhelm for good. There will be times when life throws you a curveball, when you're going through a difficult life experience, or it all feels just a little too much. At times like these, I'm hoping that the techniques learnt throughout this journal will give you the lifejacket you need to keep swimming, but sometimes it's okay to just float while you wait for the sea around you to calm a little bit. I'll talk about this more in my final thoughts right at the very end, but for now, let's look at some more techniques to reduce overwhelm even further.

SETTING BOUNDARIES

I'm going to start with one of the most important techniques, but often one of the most difficult. Especially if you're a self-confessed people-pleaser like me! Setting boundaries is one of the best things you can do to reduce overwhelm for good and, if you struggle with this, it may come down to those 'conditions of worth' we spoke about in Part One.

WHY IT'S GOOD FOR OVERWHELM

Being able to set boundaries and say no, especially when you already have a lot on your plate, can ensure you don't end up feeling overwhelmed trying to please everybody all at once. A boundary makes us feel safe because we know what to expect when we've set those limits.

For many of us, however, it can feel almost wrong to set boundaries with people. If you're the kind of person that likes to help everyone and be there for those you love, then you may worry that saying no will turn you into a bad friend or someone cold-hearted. However, if you're constantly giving to others, and not allowing yourself the time and space you need, eventually you will burn out. In the long run, that won't be good for anybody as you'll have even less to give.

Think of setting boundaries as a long-term thing. The more selective you are with your time and energy now, the more you'll actually be able to help people going forward. It doesn't make you cold-hearted to say no, quite the opposite in fact.

HOW TO PRACTISE IT

So, how do we set boundaries that strike that balance? Firstly, it's important to establish what your boundaries are. Think about the relationships in your life right now, whether that's with a loved one or even the relationship you have with somewhere like work. Then ask yourself these questions:

· Does this relationship cause me stress or overwhelm? What aspects of the relationship causes those feelings?
· Does this relationship give me energy or leave me feeling drained? Why do you feel that way about it?
· Does this relationship make me feel safe and supported or on edge? Why might that be?

You may want to go through every relationship in your life or just pick the ones that you know are causing you the most amount of stress and overwhelm right now. What comes up when you dig into that relationship? When you know where the issues are, you can then start putting boundaries in place around them.

For example, maybe you have a boss that is constantly adding more and more work to your plate and you struggle to say no. Maybe it's causing a lot of stress and overwhelm, and is leaving you feeling drained and hating work.

This is a prime example of where a clear boundary needs to be communicated: 'I'm sorry, I'm unable to add that to the list at the moment as I'm already at capacity'.

There are lots of ways to say no without actually having to say no. What's important is that you communicate your boundaries clearly and show people that you're serious. Don't say you can't do something and then give in because they are pressuring you, otherwise they will know that they can always push those boundaries.

THERAPY

If the thought of setting boundaries is something you struggle with, or if you find that overwhelm is taking over your life, then I highly recommend seeking out a therapist that can help. Therapy can help you uncover the root cause of any overwhelm – including those 'conditions of worth' that I mentioned at the beginning – and help untangle your brain even further.

Depending on where you are in the world, therapy may be difficult or expensive to access. If possible, I recommend getting on a waiting list or applying for free or subsidised therapy (if available) as soon as possible. Even just getting the ball rolling is a vital step towards feeling less overwhelmed.

There are countless types of therapy and counselling out there, from CBT to person-centred, so look at the options available to you and pick the type that resonates with

you. Having someone alongside you as you untangle your mind and set boundaries can feel like a huge relief – and I say that as someone who's had a lot of experience in therapy!

SELF-CARE TECHNIQUES

I know that those first two suggestions can feel like huge steps, which is why I wanted to cover a few self-care techniques that may be helpful to you as well. If your overwhelm is really extreme then these should be used in conjunction with setting boundaries and getting therapy, as opposed to being relied on alone.

However, for many people, these techniques and tools can just be incorporated into daily routines to help reduce overwhelm. Remember, make sure they fit into your life! Head back to the morning and evening routines section of Part Two for a refresher on how to make these work for you.

MEDITATION AND MINDFULNESS

I used to be really sceptical of things like meditation and mindfulness, because to me it felt like something reserved for those who had the time to close themselves in a dark room for hours on end. Of course, I now know that not to be true. Mindfulness has become part of my daily life and very rarely do I need to shut myself away to practise being mindful.

Mindfulness is the act of bringing your attention to the present moment to check in with how you're feeling and what's coming up for you right now. You can practise being mindful whilst making a cup of tea, on your morning commute, or even in the shower. Just bringing your awareness to your thoughts, feelings, emotions and senses, can help your mind to slow down and reset.

Meditation is a form of mindfulness that is often (but not always) guided and can strengthen that connection to yourself even further. Giving your mind the time and space it needs to switch off from the ever-growing to-do list, even for just 5 minutes, can have a really long-lasting impact on stress and overwhelm.

TRY THIS...

The next time you have a bath or a shower, try using all of your senses to be fully present and mindful. Bring your attention to the sound of the water, the smell of your shower gel or bubble bath, the feel of the water on your skin, and so on. It's a really simple way to start practising mindfulness and a gentle way to start your day too.

BREATH WORK

Another technique that doesn't need a lot of time to practise, but can be such a game-changer when it comes to overwhelm, is breath work. For this, I'm not talking about just breathing (although that can obviously be helpful too), but being really conscious about your breath.

When we're feeling particularly stressed or overwhelmed, it's quite common for our breathing to become quick and shallow. You may even notice that it becomes harder to catch your breath or that you're breathing from high up in your chest.

Breath work and conscious breathing can help activate the parasympathetic nervous system which can help us feel more relaxed and at ease. It can slow the heart rate down and stop us feeling as though we're in fight or flight mode, which can then help us think more clearly and rationally.

You can do guided breath work alongside someone like Charlie Moult (one of the ABC's amazing breath work teachers) or learn a few simple techniques that you'll be able to do anywhere whenever you're feeling overwhelmed – like the one below.

TRY THIS...

The 4-7-8 breathing technique is amazing for reducing stress and regaining control over our emotions. It's also really quick, which means it's easy to fit into a busy day without too much trouble.

1. Start by exhaling completely through your mouth to release any tension. You might need to do this a couple of times depending on how overwhelmed you're feeling right now.
2. Inhale through your nose for a count of four.
3. Hold your breath for a count of seven.
4. Exhale through your mouth – loudly if possible – for a count of eight.
5. Repeat this cycle three or four times until you feel your body begin to settle and relax.

Ensuring your out-breath is longer than your in-breath is the key to activating your parasympathetic nervous system, so even if you can't hold or exhale for that long, try a shorter variation until you can work your way up to the full 4-7-8.

MOVING YOUR BODY

All types of movement can help increase feel-good chemicals, such as endorphins, and provide relief from stress and overwhelm. However, when we're already feeling busy and as though there aren't enough hours in the day, trying to find time for movement can be difficult.

I find it a lot easier to integrate movement into my life when it's something I really enjoy, as opposed to forcing myself to go to the gym. So, find what you love. It might be gentle yoga that feels like meditation in motion, or a dance class that has you grinning from ear to ear.

Write out a list of every kind of movement you enjoy or anything you'd like to try and promise yourself you'll get moving as often as you can, even if it's just once a week in the beginning. Here are some examples to get you started:

· Yoga
· Pilates
· Dance
· Walking the dog
· Fun exercise classes (like 'clubbercise')
· Kickboxing
· Swimming
· Cycling
· Jump rope
· Hula hooping
· Team sports (like netball or football)
· Martial arts
· Housework (it counts!)
· Gardening

And there are so many more! Bonus points too if you can find a type of movement you enjoy that involves getting outside and soaking up some vitamin D.

TRY THIS...

The next time you make plans with a friend or a loved one, arrange it as a walking date. Meet up in your local park, woods or on the beach, bring a coffee, and get moving together. Not only will you be getting lots of lovely vitamin D from being outside, and the endorphins from walking, but you'll tick off another technique on this list too...

GETTING SOCIAL

When I'm feeling overwhelmed, the first thing that gets dropped is my friends (sorry everyone). It's like my brain can only focus on a few aspects of my life at once and, generally, that veers towards work and keeping on top of my home. The thing is, however, social connection is really, really important when you're feeling stressed and overwhelmed.

If you find yourself getting into the habit of isolating yourself when you're feeling this way, consider how you can make small changes to get out of the habit. Whether it's that coffee and a walk around the park once every few weeks or even just setting aside time to check in with loved ones via text, or a call on your morning commute.

If you feel as though there isn't anyone to turn to when you're overwhelmed, you may want to join a hobby or community group that can help you build your social support network. You may not immediately make a brand new best friend who you can pour your heart and soul out to, but that's okay. Research shows that being part of something you value, like a group for a shared passion, can help you feel happier, less stressed, and find more meaningful connections.

TRY THIS...

Reach out to someone that you care about, that perhaps you haven't spoken to in a little while, with a short text or email to see how they're doing. Make sure this is a person who energises you and doesn't leave you feeling drained (think about those boundaries!). If possible, arrange a call to have a proper catch-up. It's often far easier to chat properly on the phone than going back and forth via text.

WRITING IT OUT

Finally, this is the one that I find the most effective – hence this journal! Research shows that we can process our feelings, emotions and tangled-up thoughts far better when we write them out. I can't tell you how many different apps and things I've used to try and replicate that feeling, but nothing is as good as putting pen to paper.

You may have already discovered this throughout the journal, but even just the act of brain dumping feels a little bit like relief in itself. As I've said before, our brains can only hold on to so much at one time! But it doesn't just have to stop at brain dumping. Writing is a really powerful tool that can be used in pretty much any situation. You may want to write about a tough experience you had in life to help you process it. You might write a letter to your past self to let 'past you' know how far you've come. Maybe you have a whole book inside of you that's just waiting to come out!

Getting into the habit of writing, whether it's 10 minutes of journaling every night or longer streams of consciousness, can help lighten the load on your brain and untangle difficult thoughts, feelings and emotions.

TRY THIS...

To practise writing out your thoughts and feelings, try this stream-of-consciousness exercise that's really helpful for decluttering the mind.

· Grab a blank piece of paper, or a notebook, and a pen.

· Listen to a short meditation you find online or just take a few deep breaths before you begin.

· When you're ready, begin writing everything that comes into your head. And I do mean absolutely everything!

· Don't judge whether it's worth writing it out – there's a reason it's cropped up. So whether it's a shopping list, random thoughts, or emotions you haven't fully processed yet, get it down on paper.

· You may want to set a timer for this (say 10-15 minutes) or just let yourself write until you feel as though you've got nothing left to say.

· Don't panic if very little comes up the first couple of times you do this, it gets easier the more you practise it.

· Once you're done, check-in with yourself. How does it feel to have written that down? Do you feel as though you've released something that was burdening your mind?

FINAL THOUGHTS

This is it, the final stretch! You've done amazingly well to get this far and I really hope this journal has given you plenty of techniques to reduce overwhelm. As we come to the end, I want to share with you the biggest thing I learnt through my own experiences, and it all comes back to this quote from Tyler Knott Gregson: 'Promise me you will not spend so much time treading water and trying to keep your head above the waves that you forget, truly forget, how much you have always loved to swim'.

Life is swimming, and all of the to-do list tasks are treading water. When all is said and done, will I remember that I couldn't find a clean t-shirt on the day I sat in the garden with my loved ones? Or will I simply remember the time I spent with them?

Yes, there will be things that we have to do and realistically that to-do list will never get any smaller. But don't let life pass you by on your conquest to get everything ticked off. Fall in love with swimming, with life again, instead of trying to keep your head above the waves and your to-do list ticked off.

And as I said at the start of this chapter, we'll never be entirely rid of overwhelm. If you need to do what you can to stay afloat when the sea is choppy, then that's perfectly okay. Be kind to yourself, always.

WHERE TO GO FROM HERE

While this journal may be coming to an end, your path to overcoming overwhelm is really just beginning. Before we part ways, I want to give you some final tips to help you continue on your journey...

- *Keep up with your weekly brain dumping practice.* Whether you buy another copy of the journal or just use a blank notebook, keep up with that weekly brain dump. It is the cornerstone to clearing that overwhelm and giving your mind some breathing space.

- *Change one thing at a time.* I know I've said this a lot, but that's because it's so important! Don't add to the overwhelm by trying to change everything at once. Pick one tool or technique, make sure it sticks, and then add something new. If it doesn't stick, don't be afraid to ditch it!

- *Join the club.* The Anti-Burnout Club is so much more than just a wellbeing platform. It's a community of gorgeous human beings, many of whom can relate to the struggles you've faced, or are still facing. Not only will you get access to hundreds more lessons and loads more resources to help with overwhelm and all that comes with it, but you'll also join one of the friendliest communities around. You'll find more details on how to join the club in About the Anti-Burnout Club.

- *You've got this.* Remember, when we're feeling overwhelmed, we're far more likely to be unkind to ourselves. Treat yourself with the same kindness and compassion you would a best friend who was feeling overwhelmed. You're doing amazingly well.

- *Fall back in love with swimming.* And once again, remember that life is not just about treading water. Embrace the gentle joys around you, and enjoy every second of this wild journey that is life.

BIG BRAIN DUMP
PART THREE

SORT YOUR BRAIN DUMP INTO CATEGORIES

Fill in your categories and then move everything from the main dump list into its category.

Category:

Category:

Category:

Category:

Category:

Category:

Everything else:

MONDAY

DATE:
_____

Top three priorities

1. ....

2. ....

3. ....

Any challenges I might face

....

....

....

....

....

....

How I'll overcome them

....

....

....

....

....

....

....

....

....

How do I feel this morning?

☺ ☺ 😐 😖 ☹

SCHEDULE:

☀ Morning ....

....

....

....

....

....

☀ Afternoon ....

....

....

....

....

☾ Evening ....

....

....

....

....

END OF DAY CHECK-IN

What am I proud of achieving today?

What are the biggest lessons I have learnt today?

Three things or people I am grateful for today

How do I feel this evening?

☺ ☺ ☺ ☺ ☹

TUESDAY

DATE:

Top three priorities

1. ....

2. ....

3. ....

Any challenges I might face

....

....

....

....

....

....

How I'll overcome them

....

....

....

....

....

....

....

How do I feel this morning?

☺ ☺ ☺ ☺ ☹

SCHEDULE:

☀ Morning ....

....

....

....

....

☀ Afternoon ....

....

....

....

....

☾ Evening ....

....

....

....

END OF DAY CHECK-IN

What am I proud of achieving today?

What are the biggest lessons I have learnt today?

Three things or people I am grateful for today

How do I feel this evening?

😊 🙂 😐 😟 🙁

WEDNESDAY

DATE:

Top three priorities

1. ....

2. ....

3. ....

Any challenges I might face

....

....

....

....

....

How I'll overcome them

....

....

....

....

....

....

How do I feel this morning?

☺ ☺ 😐 😵 ☹

SCHEDULE:

☀ Morning ....

....

....

....

....

☀ Afternoon ....

....

....

....

....

☾ Evening ....

....

....

....

END OF DAY CHECK-IN

What am I proud of achieving today?

What are the biggest lessons I have learnt today?

Three things or people I am grateful for today

How do I feel this evening?

THURSDAY

DATE:

Top three priorities

1. ....

2. ....

3. ....

Any challenges I might face

....

....

....

....

....

....

How I'll overcome them

....

....

....

....

....

....

....

....

How do I feel this morning?

SCHEDULE:

Morning ....

....

....

....

....

....

Afternoon ....

....

....

....

....

Evening ....

....

....

....

END OF DAY CHECK-IN

What am I proud of achieving today?

What are the biggest lessons I have learnt today?

Three things or people I am grateful for today

How do I feel this evening?

FRIDAY

DATE:

_____

Top three priorities

1. ....

2. ....

3. ....

Any challenges I might face

....

....

....

....

....

How I'll overcome them

....

....

....

....

....

....

....

How do I feel this morning?

☺ ☺ 😐 😵 ☹

SCHEDULE:

☀ Morning ....

....

....

....

....

....

☀ Afternoon ....

....

....

....

☾ Evening ....

....

....

....

END OF DAY CHECK-IN

What am I proud of achieving today?

What are the biggest lessons I have learnt today?

Three things or people I am grateful for today

How do I feel this evening?

☺ ☺ 😐 😖 ☹

SATURDAY

DATE:

Top three priorities

1. ....

2. ....

3. ....

Any challenges I might face

....

....

....

....

....

How I'll overcome them

....

....

....

....

....

....

....

How do I feel this morning?

😊 🙂 😐 😵 ☹️

SCHEDULE:

🌅 Morning ....

....

....

....

....

....

....

☀️ Afternoon ....

....

....

....

....

....

🌙 Evening ....

....

....

....

....

END OF DAY CHECK-IN

What am I proud of achieving today?

What are the biggest lessons I have learnt today?

Three things or people I am grateful for today

How do I feel this evening?

SUNDAY

DATE:

Top three priorities

1. ....

2. ....

3. ....

Any challenges I might face

....

....

....

....

....

....

How I'll overcome them

....

....

....

....

....

....

....

....

How do I feel this morning?

☺ ☺ 😐 😵 ☹

SCHEDULE:

Morning ....

....

....

....

....

Afternoon ....

....

....

....

....

Evening ....

....

....

....

END OF DAY CHECK-IN

What am I proud of achieving today?

What are the biggest lessons I have learnt today?

Three things or people I am grateful for today

How do I feel this evening?

☺ ☺ 😐 😖 ☹

BRAIN DUMPING PAGE

DATE:

SORT YOUR BRAIN DUMP INTO CATEGORIES

Fill in your categories and then move everything from the main dump list into its category.

Category:

Category:

Category:

Category:

Category:

Category:

MONDAY

DATE:

Top three priorities

1. ....

2. ....

3. ....

Any challenges I might face

....

....

....

....

....

How I'll overcome them

....

....

....

....

....

....

....

....

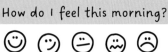

How do I feel this morning?

SCHEDULE:

☀ Morning ....

....

....

....

....

☼ Afternoon ....

....

....

....

🌙 Evening ....

....

....

....

END OF DAY CHECK-IN

What am I proud of achieving today?

What are the biggest lessons I have learnt today?

Three things or people I am grateful for today

How do I feel this evening?

TUESDAY

DATE:

Top three priorities

1...

2...

3...

Any challenges I might face

....

....

....

....

....

....

How I'll overcome them

....

....

....

....

....

....

....

....

How do I feel this morning?

SCHEDULE:

Morning ....

....

....

....

....

Afternoon ....

....

....

....

....

Evening ....

....

....

....

END OF DAY CHECK-IN

What am I proud of achieving today?

What are the biggest lessons I have learnt today?

Three things or people I am grateful for today

How do I feel this evening?

WEDNESDAY

DATE:

Top three priorities

1. ....

2. ....

3. ....

Any challenges I might face

....

....

....

....

....

....

How I'll overcome them

....

....

....

....

....

....

....

....

How do I feel this morning?

☺ ☺ 😐 😵 ☹

SCHEDULE:

🌄 Morning ....

....

....

....

....

☀ Afternoon ....

....

....

....

....

🌙 Evening ....

....

....

....

....

END OF DAY CHECK-IN

What am I proud of achieving today?

What are the biggest lessons I have learnt today?

Three things or people I am grateful for today

How do I feel this evening?

THURSDAY

DATE:

Top three priorities

1. ....

2. ....

3. ....

Any challenges I might face

....

....

....

....

....

....

How I'll overcome them

....

....

....

....

....

....

....

....

How do I feel this morning?

☺ ☺ 😐 😖 ☹

SCHEDULE:

🌅 Morning ....

....

....

....

....

☀ Afternoon ....

....

....

....

....

🌙 Evening ....

....

....

....

END OF DAY CHECK-IN

What am I proud of achieving today?

What are the biggest lessons I have learnt today?

Three things or people I am grateful for today

How do I feel this evening?

FRIDAY

DATE:

Top three priorities

1. ....

2. ....

3. ....

Any challenges I might face

....

....

....

....

....

How I'll overcome them

....

....

....

....

....

....

....

....

How do I feel this morning?

☺ ☺ 😐 😖 ☹

SCHEDULE:

☀ Morning ....

....

....

....

....

....

☀ Afternoon ....

....

....

....

....

....

☾ Evening ....

....

....

....

....

END OF DAY CHECK-IN

What am I proud of achieving today?

What are the biggest lessons I have learnt today?

Three things or people I am grateful for today

How do I feel this evening?

SATURDAY

DATE:

Top three priorities

1. ....

2. ....

3. ....

Any challenges I might face

....

....

....

....

....

....

How I'll overcome them

....

....

....

....

....

....

....

How do I feel this morning?

☺ ☺ 😐 😖 ☹

SCHEDULE:

☀ Morning ....

....

....

....

....

....

☀ Afternoon ....

....

....

....

☾ Evening ....

....

....

....

END OF DAY CHECK-IN

What am I proud of achieving today?

What are the biggest lessons I have learnt today?

Three things or people I am grateful for today

How do I feel this evening?

SUNDAY

DATE:

Top three priorities

1. ....

2. ....

3. ....

Any challenges I might face

....

....

....

....

....

....

How I'll overcome them

....

....

....

....

....

....

....

....

How do I feel this morning?

☺ ☺ 😐 😵 ☹

SCHEDULE:

☀ Morning ....

....

....

....

....

....

☀ Afternoon ....

....

....

....

....

🌙 Evening ....

....

....

....

END OF DAY CHECK-IN

What am I proud of achieving today?

What are the biggest lessons I have learnt today?

Three things or people I am grateful for today

How do I feel this evening?

BRAIN DUMPING PAGE

DATE:

SORT YOUR BRAIN DUMP INTO CATEGORIES

Fill in your categories and then move everything from the main dump list into its category.

Category:

Category:

Category:

Category:

Category:

Category:

MONDAY

DATE:

Top three priorities

1. ....

2. ....

3. ....

Any challenges I might face

....

....

....

....

....

....

How I'll overcome them

....

....

....

....

....

....

....

....

How do I feel this morning?

☺ ☺ ☺ ☺ ☹

SCHEDULE:

☀ Morning ....

....

....

....

....

....

☀ Afternoon ....

....

....

....

....

☾ Evening ....

....

....

....

END OF DAY CHECK-IN

What am I proud of achieving today?

What are the biggest lessons I have learnt today?

Three things or people I am grateful for today

How do I feel this evening?

TUESDAY

DATE:

Top three priorities

1. ....

2. ....

3. ....

Any challenges I might face

....

....

....

....

....

....

How I'll overcome them

....

....

....

....

....

....

....

How do I feel this morning?

☺ ☺ 😐 😵 ☹

SCHEDULE:

☀ Morning ....

....

....

....

....

☀ Afternoon ....

....

....

....

....

☽ Evening ....

....

....

....

END OF DAY CHECK-IN

What am I proud of achieving today?

What are the biggest lessons I have learnt today?

Three things or people I am grateful for today

How do I feel this evening?

WEDNESDAY

DATE:

Top three priorities

1. ....

2. ....

3. ....

Any challenges I might face

....

....

....

....

....

....

How I'll overcome them

....

....

....

....

....

....

....

SCHEDULE:

☀ Morning ....

....

....

....

....

....

☀ Afternoon ....

....

....

....

....

....

☾ Evening ....

....

....

....

END OF DAY CHECK-IN

What am I proud of achieving today?

What are the biggest lessons I have learnt today?

Three things or people I am grateful for today

How do I feel this evening?

THURSDAY

DATE:

Top three priorities

1. ....

2. ....

3. ....

Any challenges I might face

....

....

....

....

....

How I'll overcome them

....

....

....

....

....

....

....

How do I feel this morning?

☺ ☺ ☺ ☺ ☹

SCHEDULE:

🌅 Morning ....

....

....

....

....

....

....

☀ Afternoon ....

....

....

....

....

🌙 Evening ....

....

....

....

END OF DAY CHECK-IN

What am I proud of achieving today?

What are the biggest lessons I have learnt today?

Three things or people I am grateful for today

How do I feel this evening?

☺ ☺ 😐 😣 ☹

FRIDAY

DATE:

_____

Top three priorities

1. ....

2. ....

3. ....

Any challenges I might face

....

....

....

....

....

....

How I'll overcome them

....

....

....

....

....

....

....

....

....

How do I feel this morning?

☺ ☺ ☺ ☺ ☹

SCHEDULE:

🌅 Morning ....

....

....

....

....

....

☀ Afternoon ....

....

....

....

....

🌙 Evening ....

....

....

....

END OF DAY CHECK-IN

What am I proud of achieving today?

What are the biggest lessons I have learnt today?

Three things or people I am grateful for today

How do I feel this evening?

☺ ☺ 😐 😣 ☹

SATURDAY

DATE:

Top three priorities

1. ....

2. ....

3. ....

Any challenges I might face

....

....

....

....

....

How I'll overcome them

....

....

....

....

....

....

....

How do I feel this morning?

☺ ☺ 😐 😵 ☹

SCHEDULE:

☀ Morning ....

....

....

....

....

....

☀ Afternoon ....

....

....

....

....

🌙 Evening ....

....

....

....

....

END OF DAY CHECK-IN

What am I proud of achieving today?

What are the biggest lessons I have learnt today?

Three things or people I am grateful for today

How do I feel this evening?

SUNDAY

DATE:

Top three priorities

1...
2...
3...

Any challenges I might face

....
....
....
....
....

How I'll overcome them

....
....
....
....
....
....
....
....

How do I feel this morning?

☺ ☺ 😐 😵 ☹

SCHEDULE:

☀ Morning ....
....
....
....
....

☀ Afternoon ....
....
....
....
....

☾ Evening ....
....
....
....

END OF DAY CHECK-IN

What am I proud of achieving today?

What are the biggest lessons I have learnt today?

Three things or people I am grateful for today

How do I feel this evening?

BRAIN DUMPING PAGE

SORT YOUR BRAIN DUMP INTO CATEGORIES

Fill in your categories and then move everything from the main dump list into its category.

Category:

Category:

Category:

Category:

Category:

Category:

MONDAY

DATE:

Top three priorities

1. ....
2. ....
3. ....

Any challenges I might face

....
....
....
....
....
....

How I'll overcome them

....
....
....
....
....
....
....

How do I feel this morning?

☺ ☺ ☺ ☺ ☹

SCHEDULE:

☀ Morning ....
....
....
....
....
....

☀ Afternoon ....
....
....
....
....

☾ Evening ....
....
....
....

END OF DAY CHECK-IN

What am I proud of achieving today?

What are the biggest lessons I have learnt today?

Three things or people I am grateful for today

How do I feel this evening?

TUESDAY

DATE:

Top three priorities

1. ....

2. ....

3. ....

Any challenges I might face

....

....

....

....

....

....

How I'll overcome them

....

....

....

....

....

....

....

....

How do I feel this morning?

😊 🙂 😐 😵 ☹️

SCHEDULE:

Morning ....

....

....

....

....

....

Afternoon ....

....

....

....

....

Evening ....

....

....

END OF DAY CHECK-IN

What am I proud of achieving today?

What are the biggest lessons I have learnt today?

Three things or people I am grateful for today

How do I feel this evening?

WEDNESDAY

DATE:

Top three priorities

1. ....

2. ....

3. ....

Any challenges I might face

....

....

....

....

....

How I'll overcome them

....

....

....

....

....

....

....

How do I feel this morning?

☺ ☺ 😐 😵 ☹

SCHEDULE:

☼ Morning ....

....

....

....

....

....

☼ Afternoon ....

....

....

....

....

☽ Evening ....

....

....

....

END OF DAY CHECK-IN

What am I proud of achieving today?

What are the biggest lessons I have learnt today?

Three things or people I am grateful for today

How do I feel this evening?

THURSDAY

DATE:

Top three priorities

1...

2...

3...

Any challenges I might face

....

....

....

....

....

....

How I'll overcome them

....

....

....

....

....

....

....

How do I feel this morning?

☺ ☺ 😐 😖 ☹

SCHEDULE:

☀ Morning ....

....

....

....

....

....

☀ Afternoon ....

....

....

....

....

☾ Evening ....

....

....

....

END OF DAY CHECK-IN

What am I proud of achieving today?

What are the biggest lessons I have learnt today?

Three things or people I am grateful for today

How do I feel this evening?

FRIDAY

DATE:

Top three priorities

1..

2..

3..

Any challenges I might face

....

....

....

....

....

....

How I'll overcome them

....

....

....

....

....

....

....

....

How do I feel this morning?

SCHEDULE:

Morning ....

....

....

....

....

Afternoon ....

....

....

....

....

Evening ....

....

....

END OF DAY CHECK-IN

What am I proud of achieving today?

What are the biggest lessons I have learnt today?

Three things or people I am grateful for today

How do I feel this evening?

SATURDAY

DATE:

Top three priorities

1. ....

2. ....

3. ....

Any challenges I might face

....

....

....

....

....

....

How I'll overcome them

....

....

....

....

....

....

....

....

SCHEDULE:

☀ Morning ....

....

....

....

....

....

☀ Afternoon ....

....

....

....

....

....

☾ Evening ....

....

....

....

END OF DAY CHECK-IN

What am I proud of achieving today?

What are the biggest lessons I have learnt today?

Three things or people I am grateful for today

How do I feel this evening?

SUNDAY

DATE:

....

Top three priorities

1. ....

2. ....

3. ....

Any challenges I might face

....

....

....

....

....

How I'll overcome them

....

....

....

....

....

....

....

....

How do I feel this morning?

😄 🙂 😐 😵 ☹️

SCHEDULE:

🌅 Morning ....

....

....

....

....

....

🌞 Afternoon ....

....

....

....

....

🌙 Evening ....

....

....

....

END OF DAY CHECK-IN

What am I proud of achieving today?

What are the biggest lessons I have learnt today?

Three things or people I am grateful for today

How do I feel this evening?

BRAIN DUMPING PAGE

DATE:

SORT YOUR BRAIN DUMP INTO CATEGORIES

Fill in your categories and then move everything from the main dump list into its category.

Category:

Category:

Category:

Category:

Category:

Category:

END OF MONTH CHECK-IN

Start by listing your top five to ten achievements this month

1. ....
2. ....
3. ....
4. ....
5. ....
6. ....
7. ....
8. ....
9. ....
10. ....

Are there any things that didn't go quite so well? Try to approach this gently and without judgement.

YOUR WHEEL OF LIFE

The wheel of life is a great tool for helping you to gain perspective on what areas of your wellbeing are going well and where you might be feeling overwhelmed.

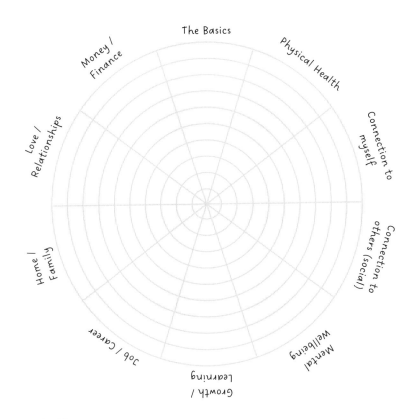

HOW TO USE:

- Visit each section and rate how good you feel about that part of your life (0 is in the middle and the lowest, 10 is the outer edge and the best).
- Draw a line to connect the dots, which will create a new circle – most of the time, a wonky one!
- The new perimeter of the circle represents your wheel of life. Is it a smooth or a bumpy ride? Are there any areas that stand out as needing attention? Perhaps these areas are making you feel particularly overwhelmed? Consider this as you reflect on your month.

CARRYING FORWARD YOUR BRAIN DUMP

Is there anything from your brain dump lists this month you keep putting off? List those tasks here.

Now, spend a moment considering what might be preventing you from completing those tasks. Do they bring up something uncomfortable for you? Do you feel anxious about them? Maybe you're stuck in 'analysis paralysis'. Write down any thoughts or feelings that come up when you think about these unfinished tasks.

Task I'm stuck on	Why it's making me feel stuck

LETTING GO AND MOVING FORWARD

Are there any of the tasks on your list that you need to let go of for any reason? For example, maybe they're just not needed anymore. Maybe they're making you feel more overwhelmed? List them here.

Task to let go of	Why I need to let it go

Are there any tasks on your list that you really want to achieve in the next month? Write them down and prioritise them in your next brain dump!

Task I want to prioritise	How will I achieve it?

ABOUT BEX

Bex, a formerly burnt-out and overwhelmed entrepreneur, set up The Anti-Burnout Club in 2021 after studying Economics of Wellbeing, Workplace Wellbeing, Mindfulness, Stress, Resilience and Burnout (all wonderful dinner party topics). She has since gone on to win two *Health & Wellbeing Magazine* Awards, earnt a Fellowship to the RSA for her contribution to reducing stress and burnout in workplaces and beyond, and fulfilled a lifelong dream by completing her first TEDx talk (without fainting) in February 2022.

Bex lives in Tunbridge Wells, Kent in the UK, with her husband Jake and two dogs, Chewy and Obi.

ACKNOWLEDGEMENTS

Firstly, I want to once again thank my incredible husband Jake who is my biggest supporter and reassures me I can do it, whenever I'm having a 'wobble'.

Next, a huge thank you to Lizzie Kaye for trusting me to write my second book for David & Charles – and to Ame Verso again for getting me in the door in the first place. You are both so patient with me and I'll forever be grateful for that.

Another massive thank you to all of the team at David & Charles for bringing this journal to life: Sam Staddon, Jessica Cropper, and my editor Jane Trollope who ensured everything made sense (I know I can ramble).

Last, but by no means least, the biggest thank you to every single member of The Anti-Burnout Club community. From our gorgeous members through to our incredible experts, and not forgetting my favourite human Rebecca Spick, The ABC wouldn't exist without you.

ABOUT THE ANTI-BURNOUT CLUB

The Anti-Burnout Club, or the ABC, is a social enterprise, passionate about improving the physical and mental wellbeing of the world!

We believe everyone deserves to feel empowered on their wellbeing journey.

The Anti-Burnout Club replaces various subscriptions and services to make wellbeing affordable, accessible and personal. Get access to over 300 hours of wellbeing classes and courses, designed to fit into busy schedules at The ABC. From CBT therapy techniques through to qigong, we cover more aspects of wellbeing than any other platform, meaning you can find what you love and do more of it.

See you there!

THE **anti-burnout** CLUB

MEMBERS

Find The Anti-Burnout Club at

WWW.THEANTIBURNOUTCLUB.COM

Use the code

OOJOURNALER

to get your first month totally free and join our supportive, empowering community.

A DAVID AND CHARLES BOOK
© David and Charles, Ltd 2023

David and Charles is an imprint of David and Charles, Ltd
Suite A, Tourism House, Pynes Hill, Exeter, EX2 5WS

Text © Bex Spiller 2023
Layout © David and Charles, Ltd 2023

First published in the UK and USA in 2023

A catalogue record for this book is available from the British Library.

ISBN-13: 9781446310663 hardback

This book has been printed on paper from approved suppliers and made from pulp
from sustainable sources.

Printed in China through Asia Pacific Offset for:
David and Charles, Ltd
Suite A, Tourism House, Pynes Hill, Exeter, EX2 5WS

10 9 8 7 6 5 4 3 2 1

Publishing Director: Ame Verso
Commissioning Editor: Lizzie Kaye
Managing Editor: Jeni Chown
Editor: Jessica Cropper
Project Editor: Jane Trollope
Head of Design: Anna Wade
Design: Laura Woussen and Sam Staddon
Pre-press Designer: Susan Reansbury
Illustrations: Annie Konst via Creative Market
Production Manager: Beverley Richardson

David and Charles publishes high-quality books on a wide range of subjects. For
more information visit www.davidandcharles.com.

Follow us on Instagram by searching for @dandcbooks_wellbeing.

Layout of the digital edition of this book may vary depending on reader hardware
and display settings.